TIME TO TALK
ABOUT DYING

Art of Living, Art of Dying
Spiritual Care for a Good Death
Carlo Leget
Foreword by George Fitchett
ISBN 978 1 78592 211 4
eISBN 978 1 78450 491 5

Chaplaincy in Hospice and Palliative Care
Edited by Karen Murphy and Bob Whorton
Foreword by Baroness Finlay of Llandaff
ISBN 978 1 78592 068 4
eISBN 978 1 78450 329 1

Spirituality in Hospice Care
How Staff and Volunteers Can Support the Dying and Their Families
Edited by Andrew Goodhead and Nigel Hartley
Foreword by the Rt Revd Dr Barry Morgan
ISBN 978 1 78592 102 5
eISBN 978 1 78450 368 0

TIME TO TALK ABOUT DYING

How Clergy and Chaplains Can Help Senior Adults Prepare for a Good Death

Fred Grewe

Jessica Kingsley *Publishers*
London and Philadelphia

First published in 2018
by Jessica Kingsley Publishers
73 Collier Street
London N1 9BE, UK
and
400 Market Street, Suite 400
Philadelphia, PA 19106, USA

www.jkp.com

Library of Congress Cataloging in Publication Data
A CIP catalog record for this book is available from the Library of Congress

British Library Cataloguing in Publication Data
Names: Grewe, Fred, author.
Title: How clergy and chaplains can help senior adults prepare for a good death by addressing it now : the soul's legacy / Fred Grewe.
Description: London ; Philadelphia : Jessica Kingsley Publishers, 2018. | Includes bibliographical references.
Identifiers: LCCN 2017058730 | ISBN 9781785928055 (alk. paper)
Subjects: | MESH: Attitude to Death | Aged--psychology | Aging--psychology | Patient Preference--psychology | Pastoral Care--methods | Clergy
Classification: LCC R726.8 | NLM WM 61 | DDC 616.07/8--dc23
LC record available at https://lccn.loc.gov/2017058730

ISBN 978 1 78592 805 5
eISBN 978 1 78450 846 3

Printed and bound in the United States

for Eli

Contents

Acknowledgments

A preacher once wrote, "All wisdom is plagiarism; only stupidity is original" (Kerr 1988, p.1). By that measure I confess any wisdom contained in these pages has certainly been obtained by others, and I have given credit where I can remember from whom I accessed it. The original ideas can be attributed to me. With that said, there are a good number of people who have generously aided and supported me in this ongoing project, and I owe them deep thanks.

To Rey and Darla DeVera who made my academic career possible by their faith, trust, and financial support.

To my so-very-kind dissertation committee: Doctors Jim Lawrence, Dorsey Blake, and Randy Miller.

To Fathers Jim and Joel, Doctors Michael and Prakash, and dear friends Dee Anne, Jerry, and Dorothy, who lent listening ears and offered probing questions to help shape this project.

To my dear friend Luke.

To my incredibly gifted and understanding colleagues at Providence Hospice who inspire me to do my best work every day.

To Dr. George Fitchett and Natalie Watson for their extraordinary kindness.

To the brave souls from the First Congregational United Church of Christ in Ashland, Eastwood Baptist Church, and the Rogue Valley Manor who were willing participants in the original groups making this project possible. The depth of honesty and vulnerability they so freely shared have turned what was simply an idea into a life-giving experience.

And most importantly to the nearly 2000 dear human beings who have allowed me into their final days to share their hopes, dreams, fears, regrets, loves, and lives–and have been my beloved tutors for this shared journey we call life.

Introduction

I meet people right where they sleep. I find them, often unconcerned about their appearance, lying or sitting on their beds in homes, adult foster homes, assisted living facilities, nursing homes, or memory care units. A doctor has told them they have less than six months of life. Many require aid to simply breathe. During my visit a concentrator frequently swooshes in the background delivering needed oxygen through a plastic tube into the cannula placed at the entry of their nostrils.

I am a hospice chaplain.

Often the people I meet are overwhelmed. Overwhelmed by the dire news given by their doctor. Overwhelmed by pain and/or the side effects of the narcotics they are on–or both. Often constipated. Overwhelmed by the invasion of hospice workers who have five working days to complete government-mandated initial assessments. Overwhelmed by the same questions over and over again. Overwhelmed by the shock and tears of loving friends and family. Overwhelmed by the knowledge that soon they will cease to be.

The waiting is awful. They know something is going to happen... something not good...and they don't know when. They know it's coming, just not when it's coming.

Some folks try to take care of as many personal life details as possible. Some get angry. Some just give up. Many just stare out the window in shock, trying to make sense of so many stitched-together memories, shaping those fragments into something that resembles meaning.

In the past 12 years I have journeyed with nearly 2000 folks who have died. On an average week I visit 20 to 25 terminal patients, and in my current job I see about 70 different people each month. Over 300 of my patients die each year.[1]

I generally don't tell people what I do for a living. I mean, when you tell someone you are a hospice chaplain, they tend to just tilt their head knowingly and look at you with big doe eyes like you're Brother Teresa.

And I'm not.

It's not that I don't love what I do or am not proud of it. Actually, I find my work both quite inspiring and refreshing. Inspiring because of the courage and strength I witness every day by patients and family members. Refreshing in that I encounter very little in the way of nonsense. By the time I get to meet our patients most of the nonsense has been kicked out of them–either by a doctor's terminal diagnosis or by some painfully failed therapy–or both.

Clergy by and large have to put up with a lot of nonsense. I sure did when I was a pastor. It usually sounds something like this: "Why do we have to sing the same songs every Sunday?" or "You know, if we could just get out 15 minutes earlier we could beat the Baptists to all the good restaurants" or "That was a wonderful sermon pastor, one of your best!" Pure nonsense.

Hospice patients know they don't have time for such silliness. Every alert minute takes on profound importance when you know there are precious few left. I find the brutal honesty of conversations with such people incredibly rich and refreshing. There's so little pretense, so little posturing. The sacredness of such moments demands my full attention and it feels as though time simply stands still in silent homage.

That's not to say such conversations are always serious. They're not. But what they are is honest.

For example, I remember when Carolyn was telling me about how depressed she became after her doctor told her her cancer was inoperable and she only had a few months of life left.

1   These opening paragraphs first appeared in my article "Healing in hospice," published by *PlainViews* in 2013, and are used here with permission.

"I stayed in bed for three or four days just crying," she said. "I didn't get dressed or shower–I just cried. Then one morning my daughter Jennifer came in and brought me breakfast. I started yelling at her that I didn't want any God damned food, and if I'da had a bag I'd just put it over my head and end it all right now!

"'Paper or plastic?' Jennifer asked.

"Well, how can you stay depressed when someone treats you like that? So I got up and ate and decided to continue living until I can't anymore."

Such folks are daily reminders for me to live intentionally now–while I can. Because the reality is none of us is promised tomorrow.

The wisdom imparted by brave souls like Carolyn has informed and formed not only my practice of chaplaincy but many of the concepts in this book. I've included narratives from the lives of patients not only to ground the theory presented in real-life situations but also as a way of honoring what they have taught me. While changing superficial identifiers and sometimes building a composite from several different patients, I have attempted to capture and communicate the wisdom these adventurers on the threshold of eternity have to offer.

Dame Cicely Saunders, the founder of the modern hospice movement, has said:

> The answer to the question of the preparation for this kind of work is that *you learn the care of the dying from the dying themselves*. But only if you look at them with respect and never merely with pity, and allow them to teach you. It is they who show us that the fear of death is overcome. Seeing this, we, too, can come to the place [where]..."we cannot know what is beyond the end of our days, but we can enter into an order of things which can make us say, 'I'm not afraid.'" (Pearson 1969, p.78)

These beautifully insightful words offer us a challenge and a hope. The challenge is there are some things we can only learn by the doing. And the hope is we will be radically changed by what we learn. One of my early pastoral mentors had a similar message: some things are just better caught than taught.

So What Have I Caught from the Dying?

Of all the lessons the dying have taught me, among the most significant is the power exerted by existential issues on nearly all of us at life's end–regardless of gender, education, income, or spiritual background. Now, of course, not everyone has struggles at life's end, but for those who do, existential issues are most common. Sadly, these existential struggles are often pharmaceutically sedated, as our contemporary medical practices in hospitals, hospice, and palliative care don't have the resources to adequately address this pain.

Now, not one of my patients has ever said to me, "I'm suffering from existential distress, can you help?" But more often than not existential distress is the underlying pain that drives such questions as:

- Why me?

- Why now?

- What did I do to deserve this?

- Why won't God just take me?

- There must be some reason why I'm still alive?

- What is there to hope for?

- How long will this last?

- What happens when I die?

- How will I be remembered?

These and a host of other pleas like them are symptoms of existential suffering. But the real concern is that this underlying existential distress exerts profound influence over the end-of-life decisions made by patients and families. The effects of these decisions are complex, often emotionally explosive, and far reaching. Consider, for example, the following:

- "Spending on Medicare beneficiaries (the largest U.S. insurer of medical care) in their last year of life accounts for about 25% of total Medicare spending on beneficiaries age 65 or older" (Cubanski *et al.* 2016). Could it be that this disproportionate end-of-life spending is simply a response to our cultural existential anxiety?

- In Oregon, where I work, the top three reasons people opt for Physician Assisted Death are all based on existential issues, not physical pain (Oregon Health Authority 2017).

- As medical technology continues to advance, traditional definitions of what it means to be dead are in flux (Muramoto 2017).

- Recent studies have found that often the most devout members of religious traditions are the ones who want the most end-of-life interventions, and the costliest, even when futile (Phelps *et al.* 2009).

- The existential distress of anxious family members and care givers is the major cause of why a patient's advance directives are not followed (Span 2014).[2]

- Trauma is experienced by loved ones who are forced to make the decision to withdraw life support when all hope of recovery for the patient is exhausted.

- Emotional pressure is caused by shifting family roles as a member of the family system enters the dying process (Lynn, Harrold and Schuster 2011).

Like the all-powerful and terrifying Wizard of Oz who was manipulated by the little old man behind the curtain, so too these very stressful and traumatic life events are often driven by unseen existential issues.

In teaching young psychiatric patients, the famous Karl Menninger would insist that the most important aspect of any treatment plan is to get the diagnosis right (Nouwen 1986). The same is true for spiritual care providers. If the diagnosis is wrong, whatever balm we provide will be misguided and ineffective. Consequently, it is essential for clergy and chaplains who are called upon to companion with the dying to have a

2   In more than a dozen years of chaplaincy, I have witnessed how the existential fears of family members have contributed to their countermanding the stated wishes of an uncommunicative loved one concerning end-of-life care. While advance directives, living wills, and POLST (Physician's Orders for Life-Sustaining Treatment) are very important, having the conversation with your family about what you would or would not want to have done if you become incapacitated is most important.

basic understanding of what the end-of-life existential issues are and, even more importantly, that such care providers are comfortable in talking about these issues honestly with those they are caring for.

Before addressing coping therapies for these existential issues, it will be helpful to consider some of the distinctives in these two particular ministerial roles, clergy and chaplains, and what each has to offer.

First, nearly everyone a chaplain meets professionally is in some sort of crisis and this is not so for other members of the clergy. On a daily basis, chaplains encounter folks who are emotionally struggling with the hopes and fears of impending surgery, waiting on test results, in need of emergent care, coping with the physical drain of prolonged treatment plans, and even the arrival of a new baby is not devoid of emotional anxiety. While clergy do deal with all of these issues, not everyone they meet with is dealing with them.

Second, chaplains by and large are called to serve total strangers; not so for other clergy. Rabbis, imams, pastors, and other spiritual leaders generally know the person in crisis and their loved ones. Now this can sometimes be helpful and sometimes not so much–but there is a pre-existing relationship chaplains generally do not enjoy.

Additionally, when clergy provide support for the person in crisis, there is an expectation on the part of the ordaining authority and faith community that the minister will offer wisdom in line with the teachings of that particular tradition or denomination. This is not so for most chaplains. Chaplains have much greater freedom to offer insights from a variety of faith perspectives and allow the patient to work out their own coping strategies. There is little expectation that chaplains will defend or promote any particular doctrine, dogma, creed, or tenet. This is not to say that chaplains don't have strong beliefs, but it is to acknowledge that contained within the chaplain's ethical code of conduct is a promise not to exert the chaplain's beliefs onto those emotionally vulnerable folks they are called to serve. This is also not to suggest that there is something bad or restrictive about creeds and doctrines, I'm just pointing out that the wisdom these tenets hold are more the purview of clergy.

Finally, a chaplain's ministry to patients is most often short term and limited, whereas clergy may be involved in a person's life for many years. This distinction confirms my own calling as a hospice chaplain rather than a pastor. Knowing myself as I do, I can be very kind and supportive for short periods and on a limited basis. Emotionally, I'm more of a sprinter than a marathoner. And truthfully, I must confess that I am able to provide loving kindness even to people I don't particularly like by taking comfort in the knowledge that I can outlast them.

These few descriptive differences between clergy and chaplain roles are not intended to be overly generalized but simply to recognize some of the unique contributions both callings bring in support of people facing medical dilemmas. It is my fervent hope that the ideas presented in this book will enable you to provide the longstanding and life-giving wisdom of your tradition to those you minister to in a more effective and transformative way, whatever your calling.

Recently I came across two articles with very interesting and differing perspectives on the role of pastors in end-of-life (EOL) care. The first detailed a research project led by Dr. Justin Sanders in the *Journal of Palliative Medicine* which found that "clergy had poor knowledge of EOL care and 75% desired more EOL training" (Sanders *et al.* 2017). The second, in the *Journal of Hospice and Palliative Nursing* by Liz Blackler, explored how patients' use of religion as a coping mechanism impacts the EOL care they receive and the significant role pastors play in those choices (Blackler 2017). While these and a number of other recent studies highlight the need for competent religious guidance in end-of-life care, many of the innovative psychological therapies making great progress in addressing existential suffering often ignore religion (Breitbart 2003), and more importantly are often begun too late in a patient's life to be adequately dealt with.

Therefore, the aim of this book is to go further upstream, prior to the diagnosis of a terminal illness, before the onset of debilitating pain, the disorienting side effects of pharmaceuticals, loss of mental acuity, and the emotional trauma that often accompanies such a diagnosis. What is presented here are aids for clergy, chaplains, and other spiritual care providers to help senior adults explore end-of-life existential issues *while there is still time to make preparations for them, and from a spiritual point of view.*

Wise teachers throughout the ages have said that the best preparation for dying is having lived a rich life. And as paradoxical as it may sound, contemplating death is one of the surest ways to live a fully engaged life. Philosophers like Cicero have taught us: "Contemplate death if you would learn how to live" (Yalom 1980, p.163). So to aid in our work of helping senior adults die a good death we will present practical tools learned from being with the dying and research-based methodology to explore with the elderly the real issues that terrify us all: isolation, uncertainty, meaninglessness, and death. In so doing, we will be able to celebrate what has made their living rich, or begin to consider how to enrich what time is left.

My Warrants

When one approaches a subject such as this, i.e. preparing for death, it usually brings some preconceptions, biases, or warrants with it–foundational beliefs that undergird the whole project. I'm no different and feel it's only fair to share some of my warrants with you as you begin to read this book.

First of all, there is my own faith journey. My mother was Jewish (genetically, not religiously so) and my father was Roman Catholic. I was raised Catholic, became a Pentecostal preacher for about 30 years, and am now a Congregationalist (United Church of Christ) minister. For the last ten years of our marriage my wife was a Zen Buddhist. While I consider myself a devout follower of Jesus, I have studied a good deal about Judaism, Buddhism, and Daoism, figuring that if there is wisdom to be had, I need all the help I can get.

Now to the specific warrants I bring to this study. First, there is the spiritual maxim: *you cannot give what you do not have*. As you will discover in the ensuing pages, I offer a number of talk streams and questions to help senior adults consider their mortality. But if you, their minister or chaplain, are not comfortable in considering your own mortality, these tools will be of little use. Joseph Campbell has a great line: "Preachers err by trying to talk people into belief; better they reveal the radiance of their own discovery" (Campbell and Moyers 1988, p.xvi). The most significant gift we can offer aging senior adults and the teminally ill is our own sense of peace with death. Dying folks don't want book reports or surveys of the current literature–what they need and deserve is our own honest human companionship, fears, doubts, faith, love, and all. To this end, I have written with a dual purpose. While hopefully what I share will aid in your ministry to the aged, I also hope that what is wrttien will cause you to reflect on your feelings about your death. Because in the end it is you–not what you say but your non-anxious presence–that is most needed by those facing the end of their lives.

My remaining warrants are pretty self-explanatory. There is what I call the dying well paradox: contemplating death compels our living a fully engaged life now, and living a fully engaged life now is the best preparation for death. This is really the premise of the whole book and will be unpacked anon.

I believe spiritual teachers should have three core competencies: listening, asking questions, and telling stories (Kurtz and Ketcham 1992). This explains why there are so many stories and questions in what follows.

I have learned that healing is possible–even for the dying–and any work we do to strengthen a person's roles and relationships at the end of their life helps create such an experience. Specifically, I have found that there is life-giving power contained in a *blessing*. This will be explained at great length.

I believe we should work to invite people into the mystery of Reality rather than trying to solve their problems for them. We do this best by minimizing the power gap (i.e. we are the experts here to fix you) and bring our own existential issues with us as we companion together with them in this experience of life.

Now, these warrants are not a set of isolated ingredients supporting the structure of this book, but rather they are the interconnected beliefs that shape and frame my whole approach to dying well. This book is not intended to be a "Death for Dummies." It is intended to be an invitation for you to explore your own finitude, so that when you sit with a dying person you will not feel the pressure to come up with some wise words to address unanswerable questions. But rather your presence will be a conduit of peace and grace and loving acceptance connecting you and the dying in such a way that you are both transformed.

The Plan of This Book

When I first started sharing the ideas presented in this book it was in a small group format. I was simply looking for a way to share these concepts with a number of people rather than having many one-on-one and time-consuming conversations. To my great surprise, the groups bonded in deep ways and the gift of community emerged. Several folks said that they had been coming to their church for years but had not really gotten to know others as they did in the short five-week class. Numerous participants established friendships in the groups that continued for several years hence. So, while this book is written primarily for professional ministers, I hope that what is presented in these pages will also be profitable as a guide for group study.

As I've thought about why the group process is so helpful, I remembered the first not good in the Bible. If you recall, the writer of Genesis records a lot of what God sees as good–light, water, vegetation, etc.–but the first not good (Genesis 2.18, NIV) is that the human being was alone. Maybe that's because, as we begin this exploration into the mystery of living and dying, it's a good idea to have some travelling companions. Group study is not only a wonderful opportunity to explore important concepts from a variety of perspectives, it also has the added feature of providing a forum for others to reflect back to us parts of us they see and we don't. The combination of these two elements in group study offers fertile soil for the growth of our souls. To this end, some suggestions on forming a group to work on these issues is presented in Appendix A.

As will be discussed, there really is no cure for existential distress–but it does seem to be greatly diminished by simply confronting and talking about it with others in a safe environment. Additionally, any effort that strengthens relationships in the latter stages of life is wonderfully therapeutic for existential anxiety.

With that in mind, here is the plan for this book. In Chapter 1 I'll share some insights, based on the foundational work of existential psychotherapist Dr. Irvin Yalom, on what comprises existential distress and why it is so painful. Following that, we'll dig down into why meaning-making is so important, how meaning is created, and how we can help senior adults reframe meaning in the final stages of their life journey. Next, I'll present my core therapeutic idea, a *soul legacy*, and how it can help ease existential suffering for the elderly. Following that are the ingredients for helping those we care for create their own unique soul legacy and practices aimed at helping the aged cope with end-of-life existential distress: connecting with your soul, connecting with your story, connecting with the sacred, connecting with others (forgiveness and blessing), and connecting with mortality. These chapters will offer insights and exercises to facilitate honest discussion and enrich relationships.

In recent years it has become much more difficult to do this kind of reflective work with hospice patients. Often, by the time patients qualify for hospice these days, their ability to reflect and creatively engage in relationship building is severely limited due to pain, medication side effects, and mental acuity. Therefore, the final chapter of the book offers a synopsis of a program in development for churches, continuous care facilities, and study groups to help senior adults begin to explore the ideas presented here within a seminar setting.

More than nine years ago I moved to a small town in southern Oregon, Ashland, to become the chaplain for a very small community hospital and hospice. Professionally alone, I sought companionship and advice in an online chat room for chaplains. Members of the group were quite active in dispensing advice and opinions on a variety of topics. I remember one day, in frustration at my own inadequate efforts to offer spiritual care for dying patients experiencing existential distress, I posted a question asking what others in the group did to help patients reframe a sense of meaning when bedbound and nearing death.

No one responded.

No one.

Then I really felt alone.

That experience, and the feeling of inadequacy in ministering to my dying patients, ignited a desire in me to learn how to help people cope more effectively with existential distress. What follows is the fruit of that search.

1

Addressing the Existential Issues that Terrify Us All

One of my many teachers about the powerful influence of existential distress was Ruby. In her early 90s, with jet black hair, barely five-foot tall, and maybe 80 pounds, her family lovingly referred to her as "Sarge." She earned the name years earlier based on family memories of vacations and camping trips when Ruby assigned duties and made sure everything was sufficiently prepared for the adventure. I think the name was earned by her attitude as much as her function.

To say Ruby had lived a colorful life is inadequate. Part of her résumé included being a snake charmer at carnival side shows and a Pentecostal preacher with her own radio program.

I had first met Ruby several years prior when her husband was on our hospice service. At her urging he had agreed to get baptized. She wanted to make sure he would be waiting for her in the right place on the other side. I drove out to their cabin in the rural woods of southern Oregon and provided the sacrament under the watchful eye of several stuffed cobras, mementos from Ruby's carnival days.

Now it was Ruby's turn for hospice care, and she was struggling. As she was now bedbound, her son and his wife moved a camper onto Ruby's little property to provide 24/7 care.

On my first visit after catching up on her life since her husband's death, Ruby began to bark out her complaints: "Why am I still here?

Why won't God take me? I'm ready to die... I've lived a good life. I'm ready to go! What's taking God so long?"

I looked her right in the eye and told her, "Look, you know I've been a minister for over 40 years, and if there's one thing I've learned it's this–God is horrible..." She was stunned and I had her full attention. "God is horrible Sarge, *at taking orders*." She laughed hard. I continued, "Ruby, I've tried to teach God how to take orders. I really have. I've screamed, and yelled, and threatened–it just doesn't work. God shows no interest to learn." She smiled knowingly.

That short conversation helped alleviate her existential pain for a little while. But when I returned in a few weeks, it was back.

"I'm ready to go. Why won't God take me? I hate just laying here and waiting..." Ruby complained.

"Look, here's the reality. You're dying, and that stinks. But, you're not in pain, you're on a comfortable bed in your own home, you're safe and warm, and the people who love you most are caring for you. At this time of life, Ruby, it just doesn't get any better than this. Quit your bitchin'."

After the momentary shock on her face disappeared, she laughingly said, "Thanks, I needed that."

Like so many folks I visit, Ruby was suffering from existential distress. So, what is meant by this mysterious and off-putting phrase *existential distress*? Much of my own thinking on this topic has been informed and colored by the wisdom of Dr. Irvin Yalom. His classic work *Existential Psychotherapy* is a rich book with easily accessible insights that is well worth the effort. Yalom teaches that existential distress is a combination of four basic human fears: isolation, freedom, meaninglessness, and death (see Figure 1.1).

Yalom asserts that these four fears are universal and wax and wane in terms of severity over the course of our lives. As a psychiatrist, he believes every person coming to see him professionally is really struggling with one or more of these issues, but because they are so terrifying, his patients often make up other problems that are more manageable to avoid addressing these. I have learned that with the onset of a terminal diagnosis our defense mechanisms are shattered, and we no longer have the resources to hide from these profoundly human questions.

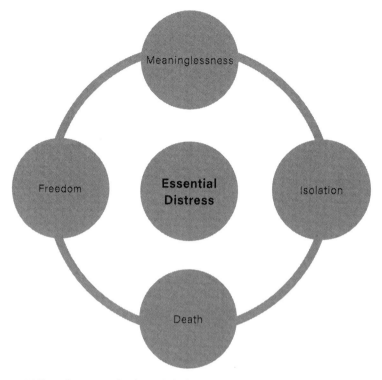

Figure 1.1 Four Sources of Existential Distress (Yalom 1980)

The Value of Existential Pain

Before taking a look at some of the symptoms of existential pain, I'd like to suggest some of its benefits. Yes, I believe there is value in existential suffering.

First of all, pain is a can't-ignore message that we have a problem. It is our body's way of letting us know that something is drastically wrong and requires immediate attention. This is not a back-burner issue or something that can wait for later. And as any good Twelve Stepper (Alcoholics Anonymous member) can tell you, before you can change anything you have to admit there is a problem.

In fact, pain is a very effective change agent. Most of us know that we shouldn't smoke and that we should eat balanced diets and exercise regularly. We are well informed. We know what to do. We just find it so difficult to make those changes necessary for our better health. We watch inspiring videos, we go to conferences, yet long-lasting change remains elusive. But pain has a way of kicking change into gear. Think about the most significant changes you've made over the course of your life–I'll bet most of them occurred during or just after very painful periods.

Simply put, pain is a call to wake up.

Now, existential pain is a particular type of pain that has specific benefits. For instance, it is really effective at shattering our false illusions of self-importance and invites us into reality. As will be discussed at length in Chapter 5, one of the most human of projects is to create a story of who we are and why we are. We all do it. In this story-crafting enterprise we often tend to overestimate our importance in the grand cosmos. Existential pain uses blunt force to shatter these illusions of our being the very center of the universe and beckons us into the unknown and unpredictable experience of reality. And it is *only* in reality that authentic living can be experienced.

How does it do this? By providing an opportunity to focus on what is truly important. It might seem paradoxical, but as we honestly wrestle with the choices we've made, the roles and relationships that have given us meaning, and our attitudes concerning death, we discover fertile soil for living deeply in the years still ahead.

Another significant aspect of existential pain is that it is *normal* at life's end. Harvey Chochinov, one of the leading researchers in existential end-of-life care, has observed, "Existential confrontation with approaching death raises many questions: What is the meaning of my existence? What has my life amounted to? And, as a pressing concern: Once I am gone, what difference will my life have made?" (2012, p.16). These are the types of questions the dying should be wrestling with.

And existential pain's final benefit? It reminds us that we are alone.

Isolation

On Monday, a few weeks before Christmas, I visited three people.

The first was a woman who has battled MS for most of her life. Now bedbound with great difficulty in swallowing, when I asked what she wanted prayer for, she replied, "I want to be married. I want to be loved." I prayed, knowing full well that'll never happen.

A really nice woman with a quick mind and teasing sense of humor trapped in a body that has never worked well. Her soul longs to be special. To be desired. To be loved.

Next I visited a young man (in his 30s) who was born addicted to drugs. Mom was a meth addict. He was emotionally on the level of an eight-year-old and terribly afraid of dying. Painful wounds on his buttocks that wouldn't heal. Ashen white skin wrapping his protruding bones.

When I showed up he was out in the courtyard of the facility, smoking. Shortly into my visit his mom arrived. He immediately reached with both arms from his wheelchair and tearfully cried, "Mommy." She had brought him a hamburger with no onions from McDonald's...his favorite.

A life of drug use has left him with few teeth, so my patient was reduced to merely sucking on the burger rather than biting it. Mom stood by and dutifully squirted ketchup on it between sucks.

Several friends and an aunt joined us in the courtyard. The sky was blue, the sun was shining, but it was cold. Everybody smoked but me. It was awkward. We were together but alone. These folks who knew each other well and loved each other were on polite behavior as I, a relative stranger and supposed man of God, was in their midst.

I tried to be nice, made a few attempts at conversation, and encouraged them in their love and care for my patient. But it was awkward. They were too nice to just say, "Go sell crazy somewhere else...we're all full up here."

My final visit was with a woman in her 90s who can no longer remember who she is, or where she is, or why she is. Mercifully she was soundly asleep, saving us both from the uncomfortable chore of trying to converse, so I just sat silently and prayed blessings for her. Praying however she and God communicate, even in a broken-down body with a short-circuited mind, that Yahweh would remind her she is loved and of the promise that the Holy One will never leave or forsake her (Hebrews 13.5b, NIV).

The next morning as I was thinking about these folks, and praying for them, I became keenly aware of how alike we all are. These three dying folks and me. The details of my life are a little different but we all share hopes and dreams that will never happen. We all have experienced painful disappointments. We all ache to be loved. To feel special. We often feel all alone, living awkwardly in a world that has no place for us. Frightened lost souls looking for a place to fit.

Somewhere in my praying and thinking, words from Merton surfaced into my consciousness:

> Thank God, thank God that I *am* like other men, that I am only a man among others... I have the immense joy of being a man, a member of a race in which God Himself became incarnate. As if the sorrows and stupidities of the human condition could overwhelm me, now I realize what we all are. And if only everybody could realize this! But it cannot be explained. There is no way of telling people that they are all walking around shining like the sun. (Merton 1968, p.157)

So the question that begs the asking is, why would God want to become human? For love, certainly. But why specifically?

In the Garden story after the first man and woman felt ashamed, God screamed out, "*Where are you?*" Did God come to find us? To let us know that we are not *alone*? To help us find our way home? To demonstrate in the most dramatic fashion that we are accepted? Is this the real present Christmas offers?

If so, maybe we are most God-like when we simply reach out to another lost soul and communicate, "I am with you."

The dying have taught me that such feelings of intense aloneness that randomly overwhelm us can also become the pathway to our connectedness. My encounters with such seemingly isolated individuals, people who are in pain and nearing death, touch my own experience of isolation and often create a space for deeper human connection, thereby calming the cry of isolation in both of us.

But pain is an ambiguous messenger. In his insightful book *The Language of Pain*, physician David Biro explores why diagnosing pain is so difficult for doctors–doctors can't feel our pain. Pain is "the quintessential private experience" because it "underscores our separateness from other people" (2010, p.19). So we try, using metaphors, to explain what the pain is like: "It's like a sharp stabbing knife in my right side" or "My head is throbbing so bad it feels like it could explode." We struggle to communicate what the pain feels like because we are the only one who feels it. We are alone.

And then there is the ultimate experience of isolation–death. With his usual ironic twist, Thomas Merton puts it this way: "Death makes this very clear, for when a man dies, he dies alone. The only one for whom the bell tolls, in all literal truth, is the one who is dying" (Merton 1976, p.167). Pain, suffering, death–all combine to unearth one of our deepest fears. They remind us that in this vast expansive universe we are ultimately, and absolutely, alone.

Freedom

Now at first blush you may be wondering how *freedom* can add to existential distress. After all, doesn't everybody want freedom? But as existential philosophers will tell you, there is an aspect of freedom that is downright scary–that is its uncertainty.

We live in a time when there are so many choices to be made, how do we know which one is best? For example, getting a cup of coffee these days is an existential nightmare. Forty years ago you ordered coffee, and there were two choices, cream or sugar. Today the possibilities are exhausting: soy, almond, whole, half and half, or 2 percent milk, and then there are at least four types of non-calorie sweeteners. All of this factors into the relatively simple decision to order a cup of coffee. What about the bigger life questions? How can I be sure I married the right person? Did I pick the right career? Should I move to another place? Rent or own? How can I be sure?

In the healthcare world these freedoms are not only frightening but debilitating as well. Should I do the chemo? The radiation? What about surgery? Non-traditional approaches? Untested new therapies? Tens of thousands of families are torn apart each year trying to come to consensus on these and a host of other medical decisions. So many of the exhausted hospice patients I serve have family members who are angry at them for "giving up." How do we know when enough is enough?

And yet in the midst of all this uncertainty, we must choose. So many of the patients I have served have taught me that the choices we make and how we make them deeply affect our experience of living. Patients like Robert.

The highlight of my week was hearing Robert say, "Hi Fred."

I couldn't quite figure Robert out. He was a kind man living in a body that was just wearing out. From the stuff in his room at the Adult Foster

Home, I knew Robert loved his family, the Dallas Cowboys, and the Blues Brothers.

His son told me that Robert used to play the electric bass and sing in a rock band. He'd always loved music, and like another musician, Woody Guthrie, Robert was dying of Huntington's disease. He'd lost most of his muscle control, his little body spasmed awkwardly, and he struggled mightily just to get a word or two out.

Every time I'd visit I always asked if he was in pain. He always said, "No." I asked him about the care he received. "It's good," he replied. Any complaints? "No."

Sitting there praying for Robert, watching him spasm awkwardly, and seeing the peace in his eyes–I thought about Sisyphus.

If you remember your Greek mythology, Sisyphus was the man who got stuck for all eternity rolling the big rock up the hill, only to have it roll back down every time he got it up there. For me, Sisyphus is Exhibit A of *futility*. But not so for Albert Camus. For Camus, Sisyphus was a hero.

In his essay "The Myth of Sisyphus," Camus wrote that Sisyphus loved rolling that big rock up the hill because it reminded Sisyphus *he was alive*. The feel of the cold stone on his face, the heavy weight pushing against the muscles in his arms and legs, the cool air his lungs inhaled to muster the energy to move that big rock all told Sisyphus *he was real and he was alive*. And for Sisyphus that was enough. That being was better than not being.

So as I would sit next to Robert praying for him I thought about Sisyphus. Somehow Robert made peace with his decaying physical condition. It's my worst nightmare–being trapped in a body that won't work. But Robert didn't complain or show any sign of annoyance. He *chose* to be pleasant and kind. As I say, I couldn't quite figure Robert out.

Maybe like Camus' Sisyphus, Robert simply loved being. Maybe he knew that one day soon enough he would be gone from this "mortal coil." Maybe Robert had discovered the secret of just enjoying each moment of life he had been given regardless of the circumstances?

I don't know. But I can tell you, Robert sure made me feel very special when I walked into his room and saw him struggle so to simply gurgle out, "Hi Fred." He made me feel very glad to be alive.

Having to make choices in an uncertain universe is terribly daunting. And yet, like Robert, we must choose. How people make these choices is very personal. Some rely on faith. Some on accumulated life wisdom. Some on advice from loved ones. But I have come to learn that those who can make these uncertain choices from a place of surrender to the reality of their situation and acceptance die a much more peaceful death.

Meaninglessness

My first experience in observing the intense pain caused by a loss of meaning at life's end came long before my career as a chaplain began; it began with watching my mother die.

She was only 44 and had battled cancer for seven years. It started in her breast, then went to the ovaries, then finally and painfully into her bones. Double mastectomy, hysterectomy, chemo, radiation, the indignity of all her beautiful black hair falling out, her caring face mooning up from the medications–none of it worked. For the last year of her life she basically lay in pain on the couch in our family room and had to let my three sisters, my father, and I care for her every need.

The greatest pain she endured, though, was not being able to be our mom anymore. She often told me she hated having everyone wait on her. She felt like such a burden to us. For all our life she had cared for and nurtured us–now she could only lie on that damn couch.

I remember one evening during her last year, she and I were home alone. I was lying on the floor in the family room watching TV and she asked me, "Do you want some ice cream?" Half jokingly I said, "Yeah, right."

A short while later she labored to get up off of the sofa, grabbed her crutches, and started up the seven stairs from the family room to the rest of the house. I thought she was just going to the bathroom. She returned gingerly balancing a bowl of ice cream in her right hand, walking with the crutches, and cautiously making her way back down the seven stairs. I felt so ashamed, and yet she looked so happy. For just a few moments, she told me she felt like a mom again.

Conversely, those were some of the richest moments in my life. I had just graduated from college and moved home to help care for her. Those last several months of tending to my mother were an opportunity for me to give back to this beautiful woman who had given me and our family so much of herself. Serving her pulled a kindness and sensitivity out of me that I didn't even know was there. I was a better human being as a result of those months spent caring for my dying mother.

Ironically, letting us serve her as she was dying was the final gift our mother gave us. Her care filled *our* lives with deep meaning. Now I'm not suggesting it was easy, or that it made us happy, but it did make our living very rich. Frequently I share this insight with those I serve who also suffer from a loss of meaning as they lie dying. I suggest that dying patients, even confined to their hospital beds and unable to care for themselves, can still teach the rest of the family how meaningful life can be in serving others.

Nearly 40 years later, the impact of those months has never left me. The experience of caring for my dying mother was a major factor in my decision to become a hospice chaplain (Grewe 2014, pp.111-113).

Leading research reveals that for those dying like my mother, for those who are suffering, a sense of meaning has therapeutic power to alleviate the existential pain (Chochinov 2012).

Having a clearly defined sense of purpose and meaning is an effective balm to soothe the soul as it is in the process of being dislocated from a diminishing body. One of the ways a sense of meaning relieves this suffering is by buffering the dying person from the effects of what I call the great North American mortal sin–*becoming a burden to others*. As in my mother's case, and for many of the people I have served over the years, the fear of becoming a burden to loved ones is the cause of intense existential pain. Numerous studies verify that this *burden to others* fear is "associated with a loss of will to live, a desire for death, and outright requests for euthanasia or assisted suicide" (Chochinov 2012, pp.32-33). It is the shadow side of our culture's obsession with and idolization of *independence*.

Without question, helping patients reframe a sense of meaning at life's end is the most frequent need I encounter with hospice patients. But this work is difficult and can open up serious introspection for the care providers as well, as I discovered with Annette.

Annette had a well-traveled life of pleasure seeking which at 78 left her with lung cancer, cirrhosis of the liver, a very painful cough, and being tethered to oxygen tubing.

Her only family was a stepson who raided her bank account before taking off for parts unknown. As a result, Annette's home went into foreclosure, and she was evicted. I met her at a Skilled Nursing Facility (SNF), and she was unusual in that she is one of the few folks I have ever met who actually enjoyed being in an SNF. Having been a prisoner in her own home alone for so long, due to the needed oxygen and her inability to get around on legs that worked intermittently, she really enjoyed having people to talk to.

A likeable gal who loved to tease, Annette was fun to visit. At our first meeting, I remember she told me that even though she knew she was dying she didn't want to be on hospice care and wanted all heroic measures employed to keep her alive. When I asked her why she wanted to live–given she had no real family, she was enduring severe pain from an incurable cough, she had no ability to get out of bed unaided or toilet herself alone–her response floored me: "I just downloaded Windows 10 on my laptop and I've reached the gold medal level on solitaire wins and I want to make diamond."

I tried hard to not look stunned.

Judgmental thoughts screamed inside my head like, "You're willing to spend hundreds of thousands of Medicare dollars on emergency room visits and ICUs just so you can reach diamond status for solitaire wins on your computer!"

But after they stormed off, another thought emerged that was even more unsettling–what do I want more time for? (See Jenkinson 2015.)

After leaving Annette I was getting into the car and that damn question would not leave me alone: "More time for what?" What am I living for? Last Christmas I got a Fitbit watch, and I thought about how many times a day I check to see how close I am to my 10,000 steps–is that my diamond status of solitaire wins? Is that my life mission, 10,000 steps a day? My golden fleece? Fortunately, there were other people to visit and numerous tasks to attend to, so that haunting question was driven back underground and out of harm's way.

For the past several months I have been wrestling with those questions, or should I say allowing them to probe me. Why am I alive? What do I really want out of living? What do I want more time for? These are profoundly human questions to ask yourself and those you serve. What are you living for? What do you want more time for?

Benedictine nun Joan Chittister is helpful here: "We are all on a quest for something. The distinguishing questions are two: For what am I seeking, and who am I as a result of the search?" (2003, p.96).

Professional pilgrim Phil Cousineau adds, "Uncover what you long for and you will discover who you are" (1998, p.13).

While I've found no answer to these haunting questions, I am happy to report that this existential struggle has helped me live more soulfully of late. I have been kinder. More compassionate. I've had more grace for all of the other pilgrims on this planet I meet who are struggling with those same four words: "More time for what?"

Who knows, maybe that's enough?

Death

One more theoretical foundation piece needs to be laid. It's an idea Yalom has subversively stated: "Although the physicality of death destroys man, the idea of death saves him" (1980, p.30). His point is that consideration of our dying actually enriches our living. Based on the insights of Heidegger and his own experience in counseling patients, Yalom asserts that often an impending awareness of death frees us from the tedious details and annoyances of everyday life and can liberate us to engage life more richly, savoring each experience precisely because it is passing and finite.

Working with numerous cancer patients, Yalom observed startling shifts and deep personal growth as a result of their physical crises. He lists most notably:

- A rearrangement of life's priorities: a trivializing of the trivial

- A sense of liberation: being able to choose not to do those things that they do not wish to do

- An enhanced sense of living in the immediate present, rather than postponing life until retirement or some other point in the future

- A vivid appreciation of the elemental facts of life: the changing seasons, the wind, falling leaves, the last Christmas, and so forth

- Deeper communication with loved ones than before the crisis

- Fewer interpersonal fears, less concern about rejection, greater willingness to take risks, than before the crisis.

(1980, p.35)

These observations align with my own experience working with dying patients during the past 12 years. It is interesting to note as well that several of the most important Christian spiritual figures over the past millennium, like Francis of Assisi and Ignatius of Loyola (who founded the Jesuits), had dramatic spiritual awakenings as a result of life-threatening experiences.

Another important aspect of Yalom's work lies in his discoveries about our defense strategies to cope with the existential anxiety concerning death. One of the two primary defense strategies he has identified is what he calls *specialness*. By this he means a hyper-individuation whereby an individual believes herself/himself to be so special as to be impervious to death. In its most extreme forms:

> The individual oriented toward specialness and inviolability (and striving toward emergence, individuation, autonomy, or separateness) may be narcissistic; is often a compulsive achiever; is likely to direct aggression outward, may be self-reliant to the point of rejecting necessary, appropriate help from others, may be harshly unaccepting of his or her own personal frailties and limits; and is likely to show expansive, sometimes grandiose trends. (1980, pp.152-153)

In my work with the dying, these traits (not in extreme forms) are very common and lead me to believe that Yalom's diagnosis of *specialness* can be applied not only to individuals but our culture as a whole. The American idolization of individualism, our obsession with looking young, our compulsions towards achievement and violence–all can be understood in Yalom's schema as one grand cultural death anxiety.

And what is his suggested therapy for death anxiety? To simply face it. Using the Stoic philosophy "Contemplate death if you would learn how to live" (1980, p.163), Yalom works with his patients on what he calls death awareness. By looking at death directly, he asserts, you can actually lessen its anxiety. But, looking at death directly is also a matter of timing, you can't force it, as I learned from Charlene.

During the first two interviews I had with Charlene she cried straight through. After fighting cancer for more than 21 years, it seemed this time the disease had finally won. Estranged from three ex-husbands and a distant son, the only man still in her life was a sometimes father she called "Daddy" and who did make occasional appearances.

Charlene was overwhelmed and emotionally exhausted. Setting appointments to visit her was almost impossible because she didn't know how to answer her new smart phone. I'd have to leave a message and she'd call me back later. She had just moved into a tiny apartment, all on one level, so she could take care of herself for as long as possible. But all of the new technology was beyond her. She had a TV and cable but couldn't work the remote control or understand how to set up the media player to watch her favorite shows.

She was a mess.

The cancer and its attending pain were bad enough, but the real tormentor in Charlene's life was the huge elephant of fear that had camped out in her apartment–the fear of becoming a burden to others. As I say, I call this elephant the great American mortal sin. It is culturally the one unforgivable crime: *being needy*.

On my third visit I'd hoped I'd engendered enough trust with Charlene to probe this painful wound. After another 20 minutes of listening to her tearfully sad story about disappointment and desertion, she began to share how overwhelming even the simplest of tasks were, like setting up her phone and the TV remote control. It was just all too much.

I stopped her short: "Charlene, you're dying. I doubt whatever awaits on the other side will require knowing how to set up electronic gadgets. So why waste what little time you have left trying to figure these things out? You're dying and you're in pain and you're all alone. You're *needy* and you'll never have these cards to play again. Look–we have hospice volunteers who would love to come and help you set these electronic devices up, and they already know how to do it. Let them come and do it for you." She stopped crying and looked at me in amazement.

"Now when they come," I continued, "look real pitiful and cough a little bit. Really look like you're dying. It'll make them feel great. They'll go home and tell their families, 'I was able to help out a dying lady today.' They'll feel like a million bucks and you'll be able to answer your phone and watch your TV shows–everybody wins."

Charlene couldn't help herself, she just burst into laughter. It was the first time I'd seen her relax and smile. We spent the rest of our time talking about how painful it is when end-of-life loss of meaning collides with the reality of becoming a burden to others. And we explored ways Charlene could reframe these feelings at this stage of her life in her situation.

I don't know that we really resolved anything, but Charlene looked better and was breathing a little easier just by talking about it all out in the open. After all, it can be so exhausting trying to hide from and not talk about the great big elephant in the room.

The Invitation Existential Distress Offers

The most effective therapy for alleviating existential distress is by working to strengthen the relationships of the sufferer. Yalom writes, "It is the relationship that heals" (1980, p.5). This deepening of relationships can be forged with family, friends, or even care providers like clergy, social workers, and chaplains.

One of the ways we accomplish this is by minimizing the power gap between care provider and care receiver. In the introduction to his classic work *The Wounded Healer*, Henri Nouwen (2010) suggests our ministry to the dying will not be effective unless we can vulnerably share our own woundedness. Our wounds can actually become a source of healing for the other. A similar idea is the theme of another profoundly influential book on my life and practice called *The Spirituality of Imperfection*, by Kurtz and Ketcham (1992). This text, grounded in the Twelve-Step tradition, beautifully illustrates how real meaningful relationship is only entered through the doorway of vulnerability, when we feel safe enough with another to expose our fears, our wounds, our failures–in that sacred space, deep communion becomes possible. I think this is the wisdom behind the biblical injunction "Therefore confess your sins to each other and pray for each other so that you may be healed" (James 5.16, NIV).

By allowing those we care for to see our own existential struggles, we can enter into solidarity, companionship, with those we are serving. We admit to the reality that we are fellow travelers on this uncertain journey and our developing relationship can become a safe haven when the night is long and the pain is frightening. Simply put, existential distress can be an invitation to greater intimacy. A place where words are not necessary.

Where Words Fail

For some patients and on some occasions words are simply useless.

Words require reason. What happens when you find yourself in a place that is un-reasonable? When the mind goes on the fritz, words become useless. Minds are very fragile things that easily go on the fritz due to disease or suffering–two things that are part and parcel of the dying process. In such a place, words are often useless. Worse, they can be harmful. Attempting to utilize sensible words in a sense-less place can be traumatizing. Words like "God won't give us more than we can handle," said to a patient upon learning they have pancreatic cancer, can just be sadistic.

Now the good news for those of us who desire to help ease suffering is this–words aren't the only way for one soul to communicate with another. There are other modes of communication. Things like tone of voice, facial expression, loving eye contact, body language, and appropriate gentle touch like holding hands all can be excellent communicators to help break the painful isolation of suffering.

But of all the non-verbal modes of communicating with the suffering I have discovered, the most profound (paradoxically) may be silence. Sitting with a sufferer, not running away, not allowing my own fear to cause me to spurt out some pithy little aphorism, simply sitting there, and maybe crying with, maybe holding hands with, the other has incredible therapeutic value–for the sufferer and amazingly for me. This is communication at the deepest, rawest, most human level and words are nowhere near. Merton has said, "The deepest level of communication is not communication, but communion. It is wordless" (1973, p.308). It is here in this wordless communion that we discover our deep unity with each other.

One of the great things about this type of communion is that it doesn't require a lot of time–but it does require being fully present. I have learned that by simply taking a few extra moments with another human being, forgetting all of the tasks that need accomplishing, forgetting my infernal cell phone, or what I'll have for lunch–just sitting with a suffering soul, breathing with them, reassuring them that they are *not* alone–is incredibly therapeutic. Some people call this compassion.[1]

Over the years I have come to learn that ministering to others as they struggle with their existential distress is not only an invitation for me to wrestle with mine, but also to become more authentically human. Like so many spiritual truths, it's simply a paradox.

So, to recap what I've been trying to say about existential distress:

- The bad news is that there is no cure for existential distress.

- The good news is that it can be diminished and made more manageable simply by honestly talking about it.

- The even better news is that existential distress can become the fertile soil for living a rich and significant life.

---

1   These paragraphs on "words" were first published in 2014 in "Where Words Fail," by *Oregon Healthcare News*, and are used here with permission.

2

The Importance of Meaning at the End of Life

When I first met Sophia, she was thrashing around on the bed in her hospital room. A friend told me she'd been a spiritual teacher for years. But now she was dying. At four-foot-something, she looked like a little elf. As I sat holding her hand for more than an hour, she came in and out of consciousness. In her more lucid moments, she taught me the three core principles of her teaching: (1) give loving allowance to those who think differently than you do; (2) give greater communication to what you truly believe; and (3) take responsibility for your own emotional health. She told me these principles had been given to her directly from "the Other Side–what you would call heaven." I knew this little woman with the twinkle in her eye had something to teach me, and I prayed we'd have enough time together for me to learn it.

Sophia did recover from whatever had caused her hospitalization and was discharged home to our hospice service. It was my joy and privilege to really get to know this fascinating woman. I learned that Sophia's father had been a Methodist minister. Sophia idolized her dad; her mother, not so much. She really hadn't liked her mother and was troubled by those parts of herself that she saw as reflections of her mother's character. Sophia had only one child, a daughter, with whom Sophia was emotionally estranged. Sophia's daughter was a born-again Christian whose goal was to get Sophia saved–a goal Sophia did not share.

Sophia was a true spiritual mentor to many people, both locally and around the country. She referred to God as "the Cosmos," and they (Sophia and "the Cosmos") were in direct communication. When I asked Sophia what she thought about the prospect of death, she responded with glee, stating, "Oh, you mean the joyous transition of leaving my body? I can't think of anything more wonderful."

Sophia's "joyous transition" took much longer than she, the hospice team, or I ever imagined.[1]

Why Is Meaning So Important to the Dying?

In more than 12 years of working with the dying, the most pressing issue I have encountered with terminally ill folks like Sophia is their struggle with the loss of meaning. My experience is not unique. Many poets, philosophers, and modern-day internet bloggers have proclaimed that we humans are meaning-making machines. Nazi concentration camp survivor and logotherapy innovator Viktor Frankl considers "man a being whose main concern is fulfilling a meaning" (Frankl 1984, p.125). Meaning-making is hard wired into our nature. Additionally, psychiatrist William Breitbart (building on the work of Frankl) notes that with the onset of death meaning takes on a sense of importance and urgency which can only be discovered by the dying person and not imposed from the outside (Breitbart *et al.* 2004).

In the latter stage of life, when our finitude is no longer simply a theory but is a rapidly approaching reality, for many people the loss of meaning severely intensifies the experience of existential distress. The result is emotional suffering. But before exploring how senior adults can reframe a sense of meaning as they age, it will be useful to have a better understanding of the distinctions between pain and suffering, and healing and cure.

Many people use the words "pain" and "suffering" nearly inter-changeably. In an effort to examine how a sense of meaning helps alleviate suffering, it is important to clarify these distinctions. Pain can be

---

1   Sophia's story was first published in 2014 in *What the Dying Have Taught Me about Living*, by Pilgrim Press, and is used here with permission.

viewed as a fracturing of the body (biological in nature), while suffering is a fracturing of the self (existential in nature) (Biro 2010). And yet this distinction is a bit tenuous, as these two are intimately interrelated. Biological pain can and often does cause emotional suffering, while existential suffering will frequently produce physical pain. According to physician and bioethicist Eric Cassell, however, suffering is the experience of distress over the assault on our intactness as an individual (Evans 2011). Suffering is a threat to our identity. A threat made very real by the onset of a terminal diagnosis.

While closely connected, the sources of pain and suffering are distinct and require different types of intervention. Far too often in the expediency of contemporary medical practices, including hospice care, analgesics, which are invaluable for relieving physical pain, are also prescribed for the existential distress caused by soul suffering. We do a serious disservice to our suffering patients and their loved ones when we simply "snow under" the dying person who is anxiously struggling with a loss of meaning. As Buddhist teacher Frank Ostaseski has so wisely observed in his care of the dying, "Suffering is not relieved by morphine. Pain is relieved by morphine" (Moyers 2000).

To properly address existential distress afflicting older adults, it is important to clarify how best to accomplish this. Simply anesthetizing it is an option—one that I suggest is less than helpful. In his *Alcohol and Poetry*, Lewis Hyde writes:

> In the Middle Ages it was the belief of doctors that if you killed the pain you killed the patient... The idea is that if you get rid of pain before you have answered its questions, you get rid of the self along with it. Wholeness comes only when you have passed through pain. (Borkowski 2012)

So what is the goal? While cure is probably not possible, healing is. And there is a difference.

Cure is a medical term that speaks of eliminating a spot from an X-ray, or cutting out diseased tissue, or using pharmaceuticals to destroy unwanted bacteria. Healing, on the other hand, requires a much broader understanding. Healing may involve cure, but it also includes regaining wholeness in the physical, emotional, intellectual, social, and spiritual aspects of being human. Healing involves the experience of transcending suffering.

One prominent palliative physician has written, "Illness and dying are essentially spiritual processes in that they often provoke deep questions of meaning, purpose, and hope... Spirituality helps give meaning to suffering and helps people find hope in the midst of despair" (Puchalski and Ferrell 2010, p.3). So before we take a look at what constitutes meaning in order to help alleviate existential suffering, it is necessary to briefly explore what we mean by the term *spirituality*.

The Connection between Spirituality and Healing

The Consensus Conference in 2009 developed the following definition of spirituality, which has become widely accepted in the medical community and is very useful:

> Spirituality is the aspect of humanity that refers to the way individuals seek and express meaning and purpose, and the way they experience their connectedness to the moment, to self, to others, to nature and to the significant or sacred. (Puchalski and Ferrell 2010, p.25)

What I find so helpful about this definition is the link it makes between our individual search for meaning and our connectedness to others. Simply put, meaning requires relationship with others.

From a Christian perspective, we were made to be in relationship–relationship with the Sacred (God), with ourselves, with others, and with creation. To underscore this point, the first "not good" in the Bible is that the human being was alone. We are created to be in relationships, to give and receive acceptance (to and from others), and to find meaning outside of ourselves.

Numerous philosophers (particularly the existentialist ones like Heidegger and Sartre) tell us it is impossible to know ourselves apart from being in relationship. The word "reflect" captures this insight. In English, "reflect" means both to see ourselves as in a mirror, and also to look inward in a contemplative way (Solomon 2000). The existentialists teach that it is by getting feedback from others about who we are (mirror reflection) that we can then truly look inward to contemplate our being (contemplative reflection). "By linking ourselves (who can't be very objective) with others (who can be more so), we gain access to ourselves" (Biro 2010, p.153). Thus the only way we can truly come to know ourselves and create any sense of meaning is by being in relationship with others.

Martin Buber goes a step further by suggesting that these relationships "intersect in the eternal You [God]" (Buber and Kaufmann 1970, p.123). It seems that the dynamic flow of relating to others informs our knowledge of ourselves and God–while relating to God informs our knowledge of ourselves and others. The importance of relating to the Sacred will be explored later, in Chapter 6.

In our efforts to heal the distress caused by loss of meaning, the importance of both our roles and relationships cannot be overstated. John Pilch, in his insightful work *Healing in the New Testament* (2000), does a wonderful job of explaining the necessity of restored relationships to any concept of healing. Pilch demonstrates that healing includes restoring the sick person to his or her familial relationships and roles in the broader community.

In first-century Palestine, sick people were often quarantined to limit the spread of dreaded diseases like leprosy (a biblical term for numerous contagious skin diseases). Such diseased individuals were forced to live at the margins of the community, and required to yell "unclean" if others approached to keep healthy people at a safe distance. Folks with certain diseases weren't permitted to live in their own homes, engage in commerce with local merchants, or go to work. These conditions increased the isolation and suffering of the afflicted persons.

Pilch points out that this is why Jesus frequently told people he healed to "go show yourself to the priest." Showing oneself to the priest was the gateway back into the life of the community. Once you were no longer deemed unclean (i.e. a threat to the welfare of the larger community), you could move back into your home to resume your role as mother or father relationally, and you could go back to work to resume your role in helping the entire community survive. This is foundational to the biblical concept of healing.

And this is not simply an ancient understanding. The World Health Organization currently defines health as "a state of complete physical, mental and *social well-being* [emphasis added] and not merely the absence of disease or infirmity" (WHO 1946).

Thus, one can be healed without obtaining a cure. Pilch adds a further insight, that "healing is also effective when the individual experience of illness has been made meaningful, personal suffering shared, and the individual leaves the marginal situation of sickness and is reincorporated–in health or even death–back into the social body" (2000, p.34).

Because of our relational need, healing is not just for the afflicted person but for the community of the terminal loved one as well. As noted in the Consensus Conference report, those providing care can also be transformed by their interaction with the dying (Puchalski *et al.* 2009). This possibility has major implications for the survivors of the dying loved one.

Within this understanding we can now begin to explore what makes our living meaningful. To begin, our concept of our life's meaning is inextricably intertwined with the story we've created to make sense of our existence. Our stories tell us where we fit into this world. And that story usually revolves around two central poles: our relationships and our roles. As Sophia's role as a spiritual teacher diminished, and her relational connections with friends and family decreased, her existential distress increased. She felt like she was dissolving.

So, What Makes Life Meaningful?

At the beginning of our relationship, Sophia was busy with visits from friends and with phone calls and emails from followers around the country. But as the months wore on, those dwindled, and Sophia often sat all alone in her apartment watching the busy traffic run up and down I-5. The traffic was a constant reminder to Sophia that younger and more vibrant people had places to go and things to do–but she did not. She was alone. Alone and unneeded. It was during this time that the Cosmos began to speak to her about "dissolution."

> I remember that she asked me to look up the word for her in a dictionary. *Dissolution* means the breaking of a bond, tie, union, or partnership. Sophia was experiencing the *dissolution* of her soul, her mind, her body, *and* her meaning. Her body was decaying, her memories were becoming progressively lost, and her soul ached to be released into the joyous transition of the Cosmos. (Grewe 2014, pp.148-149)

Now, our effort to make life meaningful draws from the totality of our lived experiences and attempts to make sense of them. Meaning-making includes "one's sense of purpose in life, the belief in the values of life, the coherent explanation of life events, well-being, and spirituality" (Puchalski and Ferrell 2010, p.116).

Meaning-making is complex, because it requires an interpretive construct linking personal events from the past, present, and anticipated future with abstract ideas and cultural values (Baumeister *et al.* 2013). The struggle to provide a "coherent explanation" is a key concept in this process. Researchers have identified two specific types of meaning: global and situational. Global meaning involves our concept of the universe, the Sacred, or God, while situational meaning is our effort to congruently mesh this global meaning within our particular life experiences. Because our life experiences are ever-changing, our work of meaning-making is always either being assaulted or in need of adjustment. The inherent struggle in meaning-making seems to be a necessary component of what makes meaning meaningful.

A corollary observation about meaning is that it is not a fixed state. It is fluid like blood pressure–it can increase or decrease–which is to say that meaning can be lost. This is one of its most frustrating characteristics. Frankl writes that while our life's meaning is always changing it never ceases. According to his logotherapy we discover the meaning of life in three particular ways: (1) by our work (our roles); (2) by experiencing or encountering an other (our relationships); and (3) by the free choice we make in dealing with unavoidable suffering (our autonomy). Frankl's insights highlight once again the interconnection between our life's meaning and our roles and relationships (1984).

Another frustrating aspect of our life's meaning is that it must be created by each of us. This seems to be one of the core tasks in living, and this work is intensified when we face our finitude in death–which often causes distress. So while the struggle to make meaning is in itself meaningful, it is not necessarily without suffering.

One final word about creating meaning must be addressed, and that is its paradoxical nature. For thousands of years philosophers and theologians have observed that our lives are most meaningful when we opt not to pursue our own happiness but instead choose to labor for the happiness of others. Frankl exhorts his readers, "The more one forgets himself–by giving himself to a cause to serve or to another person to love– the more human he is and the more he actualizes himself" (1984, p.133). This sentiment is verified by contemporary research. Karen Steinhauser and her team, who developed the QUAL-E instrument to measure quality at the end of life, discovered that what matters most to dying patients is being able to help others, making a positive difference in the lives of those they care about, saying important things to loved ones, having a sense of meaning, and sharing with family, including time together, gifts, or wisdom (Steinhauser *et al.* 2002). Steinhauser and her team go on to note that, in a recent palliative care study, "cancer patients reported that 'feeling useful' influenced whether their days were 'good' or 'bad'" (2002, p.835).

The insights of therapists and researchers such as Frankl and Steinhauser accord well with Jesus' teaching to his followers. He required each of his followers to love God with all of her or his heart, soul, mind, and strength and love one's neighbor as oneself (Mark 12.30-31, NIV). He claimed that there was no commandment greater than these. For most of my years as a practicing Christian I thought following these commands were what was necessary to make God happy. I have come to learn, to my surprise, it is what makes me happy and makes my life meaningful.

The Terrible Twin Losses: Autonomy and Meaning

> One day as Sophia and I were talking about her experience of dissolution, we began to explore the importance many faith traditions place on the ability to surrender. Surrendering

to reality. Accepting things as they really are, not as we wish they were.

So much of our existential pain is caused by this inability to accept reality, particularly the supreme reality that we are not the center of the universe. Our egos, no matter how developed they are, cling to being the center of life and are not easily displaced; yet, paradoxically, we will not find true happiness until the ego is overcome.

During my conversation with this beautiful woman, I wondered if this might be what Jesus was talking about when he said, "Blessed are the poor in spirit, for theirs is the kingdom of heaven" (Matthew 5.3, NIV). The poor have had a lifetime of experience forcing them to surrender their egos. The poor know firsthand what it is to be dependent on others, to feel like a *burden*. The poor tend to be profoundly aware that they are not independent beings. The surrender that death requires as a prerequisite to entering heaven's gates is nothing new to those who have been forced to surrender simply to survive.

Not so for the rich. Looking back over the years of my chaplaincy, I've found that the rich often have a much more difficult time coping with the indignities that dying demands. Sophia was not wealthy financially, but she was rich in the esteem she enjoyed from others for so many years. As we often discussed, this loss of status caused her a great deal of soul suffering. "How hard it is for the rich to enter the kingdom of Heaven," Jesus was also known to say (Mark 10.23, NIV).

As we spoke I wondered why surrendering seems to be the last great lesson death has to teach most of us. Is it because we will need to know how to surrender as we move into whatever comes next?

The days turned into weeks, and the weeks turned into months. I visited with Sophia regularly at her beautiful little apartment in an assisted living complex. During that time, Sophia struggled mightily with the ongoing loss of both her autonomy and her meaning.

As it turned out, Sophia would have to endure even more dissolution before her joyous transition. Because she was not dying quickly enough to appease government regulations (for fear of wasting Medicare dollars), we had to discharge

Sophia from our hospice service. Initially one might think that being discharged from hospice is good news, but folks who have received the wonderful care of a hospice team often feel emotionally set adrift after being discharged. No more nurses visiting several times a week. No more home health aides to provide baths and personal hygiene care. No more volunteers coming to read or share stories. No more delivery of needed medication to the front door. (Grewe 2014, pp.149-150)

As the disease process progresses in the lives of dying patients like Sophia, often the capacity to do for others diminishes as well, which leads to an inevitable loss of meaning. For Sophia, the meaningful life she had enjoyed was dissolving. The pain of this loss unleashed deep soul suffering. Symptoms of this suffering include feelings of meaninglessness or worthlessness in living, emptiness, loneliness, anxiety, and the dreaded feeling like a burden to others (Evans 2011).

The loss of autonomy has several key stages that I have witnessed firsthand. The first major loss I encounter in hospital and hospice work is when a patient loses the ability to drive a car. The thought of no longer being able to go where you want when you want is a major blow to the North American ego and unleashes for many the horrifying dread of becoming increasingly dependent on others. In other words, becoming a *burden*. The resulting emotional havoc caused by this turn of events can be quite paralyzing.

The next incremental loss is often the ability to walk without the aid of assistance–be it a cane, a walker, or a wheelchair. For some folks, there is also the loss of memory. As the various forms of dementia attack once-vibrant minds, feelings of vulnerability and confusion create tremendous fear. Where am I? Who am I? Whom can I trust? Am I safe? Then comes the final indignity, when a hospital bed gets placed in the living room and one loses the ability even to get up to toilet. This loss is often accompanied with the physically painful insertion of a catheter. Now, all these losses, and others along the way, come with their own pain and attentive grieving. Most folks are unable to take them in stride. They really hurt.

Recent research verifies how significant these losses of autonomy are to the dying. In one study Steinhauser and her team discovered three essential elements terminal patients want in their preparation for death:

"to face their mortality directly, *a sense of control* [emphasis added], and strengthening relationships" (Steinhauser *et al.* 2001, p.783). Even more dramatically, here in Oregon the State Public Health Division statistics show that one of the main reasons why terminal patients opt for Death with Dignity is the loss of autonomy: "Similar to previous years, the three most frequently mentioned end-of-life concerns were loss of autonomy (89.5%), decreasing ability to participate in activities that made life enjoyable (89.5%), and loss of dignity (65.4%)" (Oregon Health Authority 2017, p.6).

But as Frankl learned living in a concentration camp, while everything materially speaking can be taken from us, our freedom to choose how we respond, our attitude, is a freedom no one can take (1984). These losses of meaning and autonomy should not be viewed in only a negative light. They have a profound purpose. It seems the struggle against them is in a paradoxical way *meaning-ful*. To reap the rich reward of this struggle to reframe meaning, one thing is necessary–a protracted death. A terminal diagnosis can afford the dying person time to discern the meaning of their life an instant death does not allow (Lynn *et al.* 2011).

It is this need for time, clarity of thought, and the energy to actually do the work of reframing a sense of meaning that has motivated my desire to bring these issues forward to senior adults prior to the onset of a terminal diagnosis. Waiting until someone is in need of palliative or hospice care can simply be far too late in the process to adequately offer the time necessary for a measure of healing.

> Perhaps the greatest indignity Sophia was forced to face was the move out of her cute little apartment, with all her cherished mementos from a life well lived, and relocation into a skilled nursing facility. Sophia's last days were spent in a room with two other bedridden residents in a hot, stale, urine-smelling nursing home.
>
> But Sophia thrived in her new environment. All the years she'd invested in her practice of spirituality paid off at the end. Sophia somehow learned to surrender to her fate and found meaning in helping cheer up not only her roommates but also those who worked in the nursing home. I can honestly say that she was radiant the last time I saw her.

On that last visit, she was particularly excited because her brother Arthur was present. (Now, Arthur had been dead for many years.) Sophia was sure the Cosmos had sent Arthur to help usher her into her joyous transition. It seems she was right after all. (Grewe 2014, pp.150-151)

3

What Is a Soul Legacy?

As was presented in the previous two chapters, the great difficulty with existential distress is that it is a complex and multilayered experience. All too often the people I serve no longer have the emotional stamina or mental ability to adequately wrestle with it.

Therefore, my plan is to develop a program to help senior adults begin to address these inevitable existential concerns long before the diagnosis of a serious or life-threatening illness. To this end, I have developed a multi-week seminar to aid senior adults in the process of crafting a soul legacy to have as a foundation for their eventual end-of-life process and a gift to be passed onto surviving loved ones.

A corollary aim of the seminar is that those participants who upon reflection of their life are dissatisfied with their soul's legacy will still be able to make changes by investing in meaningful experiences and relationships while they have the health, time, and energy to do so. For, as research has shown, if we can help people experience increased satisfaction in their living, this will mitigate an excessive anxiety in their dying (Yalom 1980).

Some therapists working in this field have found what they call a *life review* helpful. The basic idea in a life review is to help senior adults reminisce about the important events in their lives and either simply enjoy the retelling or record them as a keepsake for family members.

Others have developed what is commonly referred to as an *ethical will*. This is usually a written document for family members and friends that focuses on the important life lessons learned by the dying person. It may include a life review, proverbial wisdom, and the personal ethic of the writer, hence the name. But I find the term *ethical will* confusing for several reasons. First, for most of us, when we hear the word *ethical* we think of shared cultural behavior that is acceptable, not a single individual's personal core beliefs. Second is the term *will*, which places great emphasis on it being a written document. Some folks are just uncomfortable using words to communicate their deepest feelings and can be too intimidated to craft such a testament.

Therefore, I suggest the term *soul legacy*. A soul legacy differs from an ethical will in several important aspects. First and most significantly, a soul legacy is designed to be personal for each recipient. At the heart of a soul legacy is a unique *blessing* for each loved one. John O'Donohue, a very wise Irishman, asserts that "a blessing is different from a greeting, a hug, a salute, or an affirmation; it opens a different door in human encounter. One enters into the forecourt of the soul, the source of intimacy and the compass of destiny" (O'Donohue 2008, p.199).

A blessing really is an invitation to greater intimacy. It is also much more than merely words, it is an experience. The power of the blessing experience was a lesson I learned from companioning with folks like Imogene and Bonnie.

The Blessing

Imogene had been a hospice patient for several months and lived with her daughter Bonnie in a very small travel trailer. She slept on a little cot in the midst of a forest of unread paperback books and magazines. Bonnie slept next to her mother on another cot.

Less than five feet tall and weighing less than 80 pounds, Imogene was still a very intimidating personality. She was very precise in what she liked and didn't and let everyone know it. Normally on my visits, Imogene talked non-stop (with great bravado), recounting familiar stories of her broken marriages, her four children, her years of unfulfilling work, her in-your-face life philosophy, her unrealized dreams, and her indomitable spirit. Three sons lived out of the area and out of Imogene's life, so Bonnie was left to faithfully provide the constant care Imogene now required.

Maybe it was the cramped quarters. Maybe it was the pain of Imogene's cancer. Or maybe it was just too many years of toiling at tedious, unrewarding work–but in the months I had known Imogene, I had seen how she and Bonnie could get on each other's nerves.

On one of my visits Bonnie was out running some errands, so I was alone with Imogene. Uncharacteristically, Imogene shared in a vulnerable manner the underside of her life narrative. She told me how as an unmarried teenager, pregnant with Bonnie, she had to drop out of school and was never able to formally complete her education. This was a defining experience in Imogene's life. Believing she was exceptionally gifted intellectually, but unable to gain the formal recognition, she had to settle for a less-than life. Was this why she occasionally made little digs about Bonnie's weight?

That's the backstory.

I honestly don't know how or why, but on a subsequent visit with these women at the stuffed little travel trailer I was witness to a miracle.

Everything started off as usual. I asked if Imogene was in any pain. "No more than usual," she said, then added, "But I know I'm getting close to the end...and it's OK." The bravado was absent as she began to tenderly recount the same stories I had heard on so many previous meetings. The bitterness and frustration over unfulfilled opportunities was mysteriously gone. I was even more amazed as Imogene began to praise Bonnie, who was sitting next to her: "You know, I love my sons... but Bonnie's the one who really loves me and has come to care for me when I needed her. She's a great daughter–and I'm so proud of her."

And then Bonnie chimed in, "Mom, I'm so proud of you. I'm proud of the way you never stopped learning. You couldn't go back to school, but you never stopped learning...and you've taught all of us the importance of education. You didn't let anything stop you. You got us all through."

I remained in hushed silence as for more than an hour these two beautiful broken souls spoke words of love and acceptance to each other, expressing deep words of appreciation for what is so special and unique in the other. It was a miracle. When wounded souls bless each other, it always is.

It is not too much of a stretch to say that both Imogene and Bonnie experienced healing, even as Imogene was dying. And healing is one of the most important opportunities in a blessing.

Now as I shared in the previous chapter, there is a difference between healing and cure. A big difference. Cure is a medical term that speaks of eliminating a spot from an X-ray, or cutting out diseased tissue, or using pharmaceuticals to destroy unwanted bacteria. Healing, on the other hand, requires much broader understanding. Jeanne Achterberg gives us this wonderful concept of healing:

> Healing is a lifelong journey into wholeness, seeking harmony and balance in one's own life, in family, community, and global relations. An instant of transcendence–above and beyond the self, embracing what is most feared. Opening what has been closed, softening what has been hardened into obstruction. Creativity, and passion, and love. Seeking and expressing life in its fullness; its light and shadow, its male and female. Remembering what has been forgotten about connection, and unity, and interdependence among all things living and non-living, learning to trust life. (Achterberg, Dossey and Kolkmeier 1994, p.10)

Healing may involve cure, but it certainly includes regaining wholeness in the physical, emotional, intellectual, social, and spiritual aspects of being human. Healing involves the experience of transcending suffering. At the core of the healing experience is a deep restoration with our sense of meaning.

In all of my research into what makes life meaningful, studying numerous philosophers (Western and Eastern) and most of the great faith traditions, I have concluded that what makes life meaningful boils down to just two simple things: our roles and our relationships. We find meaning in our chosen life roles (mother, father, teacher, bread-winner, minister, athlete, etc.) and in the loving relationships we form in pursuing these roles. The great paradox is we derive the personally fulfilling sensation of meaning by what we do for others. Which is why those who are sick and dying often experience an existential crisis of meaninglessness–they can do very little for others. Thus, there is a direct link between our individual search for meaning and our connectedness: simply put, meaning requires relationship with others.

So, What Is a Soul Legacy?

In this work to help create an experience of healing, peace, and sense of meaning in the final stages of life, a soul legacy is simply an instrument designed to actualize these goals by strengthening the aged person's roles and relationships. I would define a soul legacy as *any means of communicating personal wisdom and imparting a unique blessing to someone you love, acknowledging what is significantly beautiful in their soul.*

While there are a number of wonderful approaches to address these issues–such as Dignity Therapy, Individual Meaning-Centered Psychotherapy, life reviews, and ethical wills–what distinguishes a soul legacy is the central aspect of creating a *uniquely personal blessing* for each loved recipient.

In Dignity Therapy, life reviews, and ethical wills, the focus is on the person generating a document to be passed on to family members. The author is the subject of each sentence. In a soul legacy, the focus is on the person receiving the legacy. The loved one receiving the legacy is the subject. This emphasis directly addresses our need for meaning-making by attending to the benefit of others rather than to ourselves.

Additionally, a soul legacy does not have to be a written document. This helps alleviate the stress on those of us who aren't comfortable or good with words. While the goal is to communicate the wisdom we've gained over a lifetime of experiences and learning, this communication can take any number of forms. Examples could be: a scrapbook, a painting, a piece of woodwork, jewelry, a book of favorite recipes, or a collection of favorite sayings. The aim is to communicate, in a very personal way, the treasures of our heart to a specific loved one.

As will be demonstrated in the following pages, there is a place for self-reflection and contemplation to discover the treasures to be shared– but the end goal is always other centered. A soul legacy is an invitation to greater intimacy. It's like the feeling Jake Sully had in the movie *Avatar* when Neytiri so powerfully shared, "I see you." Learning how to see and identify the authentic beauty in someone you love, connecting that with what you most treasure, and then communicating this gift in an experiential way is a soul legacy.

A Word of Caution

Before I present my recipe of how we as spiritual care providers can help senior adults prepare their own soul legacies, I feel a pressing responsibility to offer this word of caution: there is no cure for existential distress, and we can't fix the relational difficulties of those we serve. If I've learned anything in over 40 years of ministry, it's this: real transformation only occurs when the individual actualizes it for themselves. We can't impose it, impart it, give it, or make it happen from the outside. Real change only takes place from the inside out. But what we can do is help create a safe, loving, and accepting environment where transformation is possible.

For patients facing death, or aged persons struggling with diminished abilities, it can feel as though their lives are completely disoriented and have taken a tragic turn. Dr. Margaret Mohrmann in addressing this experience has observed tragedies come in all shapes and sizes, minor and major, but they all have three things in common: they are sad stories; they have flawed heroes; and they represent conflicts of good and evil (Mohrmann 1995).

I have had to be reminded countless times over the years of my ministry that the patient is the hero in her or his tragic story–and I as the pastor or chaplain am not. I can't save or fix anyone. But I have also learned that companioning with another as they grapple with the meaning of their life and struggle to discern what is really important is an incredibly rewarding experience even for the bit players, like me, in the drama.

Tragedy alone does not provide an awakening. Tragedy provides the environment, the fertile soil, for possible spiritual growth. It is also the dangerous ground for depression leading to spiritual death.

As I say, you cannot impose a positive outcome or spiritual awakening onto someone from the outside. The patients must discover it for themselves and rewrite it into their life narratives. It is one of the most significant ways we honor their autonomy, trusting they will have the insight and creative energy to process what is happening to them into a life-affirming experience. Our part is to offer love, acceptance, prayer, and great faith.

A metaphor that has helped me over the years to serve folks in the midst of this disorientation process is viewing ministry as being a *spiritual midwife*. I like the term *midwife* for several reasons. First of all, a midwife is not the star of the show. All of the focus and attention is on the one giving birth. The midwife is simply a servant with three basic functions: let nature take its course, keep everyone safe, and help clean up the mess when it's over.

How do we do this? How do we companion with someone whose life is being radically disorientated and invite them into the heroic task of integrating this experience into their life's narrative in a way that gives birth to new streams of freedom, intimacy, wisdom, and compassion?

Here are a few suggestions:

- *Work to create a safe place where people can express and experience their grief.* Every interaction with a chaplain involves grief and loss of some kind. It may be the loss of autonomy as in no longer being able to drive, or walk, or live alone. It may be the loss of meaning as in "I can't be the mom or dad I used to be." These losses have an emotional pain associated with them that deserve space to be felt and explored. This is pain that cannot be fixed, but it can be held.

- *Understand that healing should include the restoration of roles and relationships.* This is far more expansive than simply cure (Kleinman 1980). We want to be a supportive presence helping patients explore how to reframe their sense of meaning and continue to thrive in their loving relationships now that they are aging, ill, or at life's end.

- *Act as a mirror, helping people reflect on the deeper meaning of the issues they are facing–but only going where the patient or family member is willing to go* (Solomon 2000). This means not imposing our agenda on them. It requires the humble understanding that we are not experts. Patients are the experts on their lives, and we must trust that they know best what they need.

- *Get to know the patients as human beings.* By really listening to them and honoring who they are and what they are going through, we can help alleviate the isolation of their suffering.

- *Invite patients into the present reality. Invite* is a key concept, as is *reality.* If we are going to encounter the Divine in this process, it will be in reality, not fantasy. We can't force anyone to go there; it must be a free choice. Some folks we serve will want a break from facing their suffering, and offering a temporary diversion can be equally therapeutic.

- *Consider exercising the prophetic role to challenge a patient's negative or limiting illusions.* This is tricky as it involves challenging detrimental self-narratives in a non-judgmental way and offering loving acceptance at the same time.

- *Realize that we are just one part of the person's spiritual care support.* We are not God's only resource to help this person. They have family, friends, and care givers who can also provide spiritual care. They are all spiritual beings. It is very comforting to know that if patients are unable to receive support from us, for whatever reason, there is still plenty of support available.

- *Give the gifts of encouragement and acceptance.* These gifts are simply grace. The receiving and giving of grace are the most important things one human being can do for another.

- *Proclaim hope.* We can't give it; we can only proclaim it.[1]

I remember sitting once with a patient who was actively dying and her daughter. Our patient was a retired doctor who had been an avid hiker, swimmer, and runner in her life, but had now dwindled to less than 70 pounds and suffered a painful cancer. Her daughter was a lovely professional woman who had put her own life on hold, taken leave of absence from her job, and had come to dutifully care for her mother.

The daughter had read in one of the gazillion end-of-life pamphlets hospices disseminate that it is often helpful for family members to tell a dying loved one it is OK to go. It is important to verbally release them to death. The daughter having read this and not wanting her mother to continue suffering tenderly said, "Mom, it's OK to go. I release you."

---

1   These suggestions were originally published in 2016 in "Chaplains as Midwives to Reorientation," by the Association of Professional Chaplains Forum, and are used here with permission.

Her emaciated mother shot bolt upright on her bed and screamed, "You want me to die! Is that it? You want me to die!"

Not the response the daughter had in mind.

What I'm trying to say is that addressing these end-of-life issues with dying patients and aging seniors is not easy, is very complex, and often quite emotional. There simply is no one or right way to do it. The ideas I present in the ensuing chapters are not sure-fire fixes to make aging and dying easier. Aging and dying are hard work. The ideas presented in what follows can be helpful resources if, and this is a very big if, we as spiritual care providers can stay fully present to the person, the Spirit, and to the moment.

Human beings are very fluid creatures. An observation shared with someone one day might produce laughter, whereas the day before it could have elicited tears. Who's to know? I often tell my patients and their loved ones, "Don't *should* on yourself." What I mean is, refrain from doing or saying something simply because you think you *should*. Rather, if you want to say or do something motivated by a genuine loving concern for the other, then it is generally a safe bet that what you have to offer will be well received.

So, as you consider the ideas presented in the following chapters, remember that they are not remedies to cure existential distress, nor are they necessarily things you *should* incorporate into your practice of spiritual care. I humbly present them as resources to combine with your own creative ministry in helping senior adults prepare for a good death.

4

Connecting with Your Soul

It was really hard for me to watch Harry die. Once a vibrant and creative man, he had been a master woodworker whose simple but exquisite furniture was on display throughout his small home. But by now the prolonged dementia finally stripped him of all ability to communicate as he lay bedbound for several years.

His daughter Constance lovingly cared for and fed him daily. She told me that both he and she were very devout evangelical Christians "who loved the Lord." Constance knew for sure that her father was "saved" and would go directly to heaven upon his death. To help in this spiritual transition, she made sure tapes of sermons by approved evangelical preachers were always playing in the background when Harry was awake.

As Harry's care needs increased, Constance had to move him to a Skilled Nursing Facility where she visited him daily to pray for his soul and feed his body.

This went on for a long time. A very long time.

On my visits I would look into those vacant eyes and emotionless face and wonder if Harry's soul was still in the shell of his ever-so-slowly declining body. There is evidence that even St. Thomas Aquinas held open the possibility that the soul can leave the body before death (Lizza 2006). What is the soul anyway? So many of us talk about the soul and just assume we all mean the same thing. Is it that animated spark of the Divine some believe we all have? Is that the *imago Dei*? Are the words *soul* and *spirit* interchangeable? When does the soul leave the body?

What happens to it after it leaves the body? These are the kinds of questions you're supposed to have answers for if you're a minister.

As I have sat with so many dying persons like Harry, they have given me the space to explore these questions head on and have graciously allowed me to admit the terrifying truth that no one really knows for sure. Oh, I know, many of us have strong opinions about the answers to these questions–opinions taught to us by seminary professors, trusted theologians, creedal statements, or sutras–but with over 33,000 Christian denominations (Barrett, Kurian and Johnson 2001), let alone all of the other faith traditions, how do we know which are right? Bottom line, none of us really knows for sure. I have had to make peace with the fact I am being asked to provide a road map to a place none of us has ever been. Folks like Harry have reminded me that I must hold very lightly to my own strong opinions about these questions and humbly acknowledge that I might be wrong.

And while I am wrestling with my own doubts and existential questions, how do I best provide support for loving family members like Constance?

In recent years grief experts have identified what is frequently referred to as *ambiguous loss* (Boss 1999) or *disenfranchised grief*. This particular type of suffering covers such situations as the grief parents experience when a child is kidnapped, or by loved ones of a prisoner of war. Families don't want to give up the hope that they will see the missing loved one again, but the one they love is now gone. This is grief with no resolution. In this category of grief is also the experience of family members with a loved one stricken by dementia. The body of their beloved is present, but their soul is either uncommunicative or absent. As with existential distress there is no cure for this type of grief. I have found, however, that simply talking about and giving it a name does give some measure of comfort for heart-sick family members like Constance.

Defining the Indefinable

Nancey Murphy, Professor of Christian Philosophy at Fuller Theological Seminary, asserts that we have no invisible immortal soul at all. She argues for a non-reductionalist physicalism–her language for humans as purely biological beings but capable of experiencing the Divine (Murphy 2006).

While her reasoning has not been widely embraced, one aspect of her argument I find very convincing. Murphy points out it's impossible to know exactly what the biblical authors were trying to communicate when they used their (Greek and Hebrew) words for *soul* and *spirit* due to the ensuing domination of the first Christian experience by Greek philosophy. In the fifth century, Augustine powerfully fused Plato's concept of an invisible immortal soul that is liberated from the body at death with the biblical teaching (Lizza 2006). Later, Aquinas developed an elaborate hierarchy of powers of the soul based on the logic of Aristotle. Murphy insightfully suggests that the biblical authors probably had no such concepts in mind when they first utilized words for *soul* and *spirit*. Therefore, we are left to read such texts *anachronistically*. She concludes that the Bible does not offer a *partitive account* of what it is to be human (i.e. body, mind, soul, spirit) but rather that we are psychophysical unities.

If you Google the terms *soul*, *spirit*, or *self*, you'll get so many hits your computer might explode. A walk through your local bookstore's philosophy or psychology section is just as confusing. Socrates believed our souls were our most precious possessions, and the key to a good life was to not harm our soul (Plato and Jowett 1930). Many contemporary thinkers argue that we have no *soul* or *self* and that what we call these things is really shaped by our culture (Hester 2010). Jung differentiated between the ego (yet another word often used for the *soul*) and the Self (Hall 1983). And then there are Buddhists who are adamant that there is no *self* and that any idea of *self* is simply an illusion (Hanh 1999).

At this point it should be apparent that defining the term *soul* is a bit like trying to define a chameleon–while it is changing colors. Parker Palmer cuts through all of this soul clutter and brilliantly observes:

> Philosophers haggle about what to call this core of our humanity... Thomas Merton called it the true self, Buddhists call it the original nature or big self, Quakers call it the inner teacher or the inner light, Hasidic Jews call it a spark of the divine. Humanists call it identity and integrity. In popular parlance, people often call it soul.
>
> *What* we name it matters little to me, since the origins, nature, and destiny of call-it-what-you-will are forever hidden

from us, and no one can credibly claim to know its true name. But *that* we name it matters a great deal. For "it" is the objective, ontological reality of selfhood that keeps us from reducing ourselves, or each other, to biological mechanisms, psychological projections, sociological constructs, or raw material to be manufactured into whatever society needs–diminishments of our humanity that constantly threaten the quality of our lives. (Palmer 2008, p.33)

I particularly like Palmer's emphasis that *soul* is what makes us human.

The Wild Animal

Of all the soul descriptions I've encountered, none is as captivating as that put forward by Thomas Merton, who compares the soul to a wild animal:

> The inner self is precisely that self which cannot be tricked or manipulated by anyone, even the devil. He (the true self) is like a very shy wild animal that never appears at all whenever an alien presence is at hand, and comes out only when all is peaceful, in silence, when he is untroubled and alone. He cannot be lured by anyone or anything, because he responds to no lure except that of the divine freedom. (Merton 1983, p.5)

The soul is a *wild animal*. Something about Merton's metaphor simultaneously attracts and scares me. For so many years I have tried to trap and kill my wild animal because it frightened me–it's uncontrollable. I don't know where it will lead. Is this wild animal the dark side, the shadow that Jung talks about?

So where does all this leave us? For our purposes, I suggest a functionalist use for the term *soul* and *not* a metaphysical one. When I write about the soul's legacy, I am using the term *soul* to mean all of one's values, morals, dreams, hopes, doubts, insecurities, experiences, wounds, fears, successes, loves, wisdom, ego, id, suffering, pain, persona, and authentic self–the totality of one's being. In my usage, the soul is the composite of a person's genetics, life experiences, and distinctive qualities. Therefore, throughout this book when I use the term *soul*, I simply mean whatever that thing is that makes me *me* and you *you*.

What's Your Net Worth?

As I was sitting with Frank at the Memory Care Facility waiting for my laptop to boot up so I could get an electronic signature from a facility care giver to prove to my boss and the Medicare folks that I really was sitting next to Frank at said Memory Care Facility, I received an ominous message from the Universe on the screen: "FATAL ERROR–YOUR LAPTOP WILL NOT COME OUT OF HIBERNATION."

On one level those words meant another ten minutes in the discomforting Memory Care Facility (after a manual shutdown of the damn laptop) waiting for the re-boot so I could obtain the coveted signature proving I really was with Frank.

On another, I wondered if this was some sort of divine commentary on my situation as I was with a terminal patient whose memory was certainly in permanent hibernation.

Regardless of the message's intent, I simply sat with this hard-of-hearing, severely demented, and uncommunicative little man with the wavy white hair in a wheelchair. As I sat, I really started to look at him. To truly see him.

Underneath the bright green and yellow Oregon Ducks sweatshirt covered with crumbs from the morning's breakfast and the matching green and yellow Ducks hat sat a peaceful little man clutching a soft pillow to his face. Frank had been a devout Baptist for most of his life, serving as an elder and deacon for more than 50 years.

While Frank's heart beat just fine, his memories and his soul had vanished nearly seven years before. As a result, this little man with the wavy white hair has little value in our culture. Oh, his biological organism is safe and well cared for, but for the most part Frank's just put off to the side, out of sight, in a memory care unit with many other breathing, vacant bodies.

So, as I was sitting with Frank, silently praying for him as the laptop sorted through its millions of codes to restart, I began to wonder if in some crazy way Frank's dementia was a gift? Did it protect him from the suffering so many of the folks I visit endure?

In our materialized, capitalist culture we have turned human beings into commodities. A person has value and worth so long as they can produce and purchase. We esteem people based on their ability to make money, spend money, or both. For example, a person can be a big jerk, but if they make or spend a ton of money, we give them great respect, honor, and attention. On the other hand, someone who can do neither we ignore. Consider the plight of the homeless, the disabled, those on welfare, or the financially destitute dying–we make them invisible.

Many of the folks I visit who realize they are no longer productive and useful suffer terribly–feeling as though they are leeches to their family and friends. Did Frank's dementia shield him from this existential and societal pain?

I left these thoughts that had sidetracked me once again from my assigned task and began praying for Frank. Lately, when I've been with uncommunicative folks warehoused out of sight from our highly productive world, I have taken to praying the last Beatitude taught by Jesus. On reading the text from Matthew 5.11-12, I particularly feel a closeness to what it says:

> Blessed are you when your life is sucked out, you're dislocated, and classified as a waste of time for my sake... Rejoice and be glad for great is your reward in the Heavens. It is a sign of the prophets to intensely feel the disunity around them. (Douglas-Klotz 1990, pp.70-72)

Seems Jesus values a human being's net worth differently than we do. I wonder who's right?

Soul Searching

In this chapter I've posed a lot of questions about the soul. Perhaps the more pertinent question is: How do we get in touch with our own soul? How do we excavate the dirt and rock of our own narcissistic false selves to discover the gold of our true beings which lie beneath? If, as the Bible teaches, we are estranged from ourselves, how do we get un-estranged?

One suggestion to help you and those you minister to search for your *wild animal* is to make a Soul Print Box (Gafni 2001). It's like going on a soul safari. Some rainy afternoon when you have nothing pressing to do, take some time to go around your home and search for five things that are most important to you. Searching is a very important part of the exercise. Now it doesn't matter *what* you choose, it is more important *why* you chose them. Place the items in a small box (if something you chose is really big like a piano, just write the word piano on a piece of paper and put it in the box). These items help give shape and contour to your soul. You might even want to share them with someone you care for over coffee and explain why they are so important.

A Soul Meditation

Expanding on Thomas Merton's description of the soul as a wild animal, Parker Palmer shares the following insight:

> Like a wild animal, the soul is tough, resilient, resourceful, savvy, and self-sufficient: it knows how to survive in hard places. I learned about these qualities during my bouts with depression. In that deadly darkness, the faculties I had always depended on collapsed. My intellect was useless; my emotions were dead; my will was impotent; my ego was shattered. But from time to time, deep in the thickets of my inner wilderness, I could sense the presence of something that knew how to stay alive even when the rest of me wanted to die. That something was my tough and tenacious soul.
>
> Yet despite its toughness, the soul is also shy. Just like a wild animal, it seeks safety in the dense underbrush, especially when other people are around. If we want to see a wild animal, we know that the last thing we should do is go crashing through the woods yelling for it to come out. But if we will walk quietly into the woods, sit patiently at the base of a tree, breathe with the earth, and fade into our surroundings, the wild creature we seek might put in an appearance. We may see it only briefly and only out of the corner of an eye–but the sight is a gift we will always treasure as an end in itself. (2008, pp.58-59)

Parker Palmer says that he became keenly aware of his soul when he was suffering a bout of depression. Psychologist Thomas Moore suggests this is not uncommon. He writes that the "soul appears most easily in those places where we feel most inferior" (1992, p.51).

Here's a suggestion to help you and those you serve reflect on this concept. It's a short soul meditation. For this meditation, I'm going to ask that you try to remember a time when you felt inferior, weak, afraid. Where were you? How old were you? What did it feel like? What part of your body feels the experience most?

Now with that feeling in tow, take a walk into the forest Parker Palmer described. Notice the trees...the fallen leaves along the path...sunlight casting beams through the branches...listen to the quiet. You spot a safe place to sit, and comfortably ease to the ground. As you sit quietly, feeling so vulnerable and afraid and alone...you simply wait. Breathe with the earth. Rest.

Can you see or sense or feel that Someone or Something appear that helped you through your past difficult time? That Someone or Something that made you feel so not alone? Is this your soul? Is this God? Is this presence strong...loving...kind? Do you trust it?

Sit with it.

If you sense that presence with you now, you might want to simply place the palms of your hands together as a reminder to yourself of what this feeling is like...being with your protector. Let the sensation of the skin on your hands touching each other remind you of what it feels like being with your protector...your strength.

Thank the presence for being there with you. Thank it for being trustworthy.

Now after that presence has departed, you can just sit and relax for a moment. Enjoy the sensation of feeling safe. Enjoy the sensation of feeling loved.

When you feel like it, you can slowly see yourself get up and begin to casually emerge from the forest...feeling energized, secure.

5

Connecting with Your Story

As I sat weeping next to Sam's just deceased body, what I missed most was the playful glint behind those beautiful blue Irish eyes. They truly were the window to his kind and gentle soul.

He had been a strapping young lad from Wisconsin camping in the Grand Tetons when Nancy and her family arrived for their vacation. Sam and Nancy hit it off straight away and, in fact, Sam followed Nancy's family back to Utah. He simply showed up on her doorstep and never left. That was 76 years ago and part of the story Alzheimer's had erased from Sam's memory bank.

Also gone was a lifetime of working for the forestry service, raising two loving sons, untold hours fishing, and traveling the country with Nancy in their little camper. Bedbound for the last several years of his life, as his body ever-so-slowly diminished, so did a lifetime of memories and even an awareness of who he was.

What did not diminish, however, was that playful kindness in those deep blue eyes. Always present to the moment, Sam loved to laugh and tease. After months of visits and simple conversations, Sam could vaguely remember my face but not who I was or why I was there. Most of the time I simply told Sam his own life story. It all started naturally enough. On one of my first visits, those blue eyes looked like a deer's caught by headlights as Sam told me he couldn't remember who he was or why he was still here. So, I just started to remind him. As I told him his own life story, those blue eyes began to water and relax. When I told him he was a good man and had lived a good life, he smiled. That mischievous Irish grin captured my heart.

Over the months Sam taught me so much about living in the present moment. That's all we really have anyway. With him, the present was all there was. He taught me how lost we can get when we forget who we are, when we forget our story–and how important it is to have good friends and loved ones to remind us. He also taught me about emotional investing. Because of the love he had deposited into others throughout his 90-plus years of living, he earned great dividends and was able to benefit from those investments when they were needed. His memory bank may have been depleted, but his emotional and relational accounts continued to thrive.

The night before he died, Nancy and their daughter-in-law Joyce were up caring for him and got no sleep. The next afternoon, Nancy had just lain down to get some rest in the next room. She told me she really didn't sleep–she called it being in a "twilight zone"–when she saw a golden luminous ball suddenly appear on the door of the bedroom. She was thinking "Is that Sam's spirit?" when Lynn came in to tell her that Sam had just passed away.

Was that luminous golden ball that manifested on Nancy's bedroom door Sam's spirit as she believes? Was it the divine spark that animated the playful glint behind his beautiful blue eyes? I don't know. But what I do know is that my own life has been incredibly enriched by simply spending hours with a good man, basking in the glow of his love with and for Nancy, and having the distinct privilege of re-telling this kind man with the beautiful blue eyes the story he actually lived.

We Are Family

Research now tells us that Sam actually began to craft his story, as we all did, within the first days of life. Studies show that newborn infants, within the first four days, can detect and react to the emerging rules of interpersonal relationships (Nagy 2008). Therefore, one of the primary and most significant sources we use to create our life story comes from our experience within the nuclear family. It is the family, the first group of "others," who begin to reflect back to us who we are in the world.

This familial influence goes far beyond our feelings of being loved and accepted, as we are named, and learn important family myths, our place within a hierarchical structure of power, and our place in the larger world. These "family stories" help shape our own personal self-understanding (Sani 2008). Research shows our position in the nuclear family unit imprints upon us expectations for ourselves and others and powerfully influences our choice of friends and most importantly our future mates (Friedman 2011). Therefore, who we are is influenced not only by our genetic code *but also by* the learned patterns of behavior transmitted to us in the primary social network that surrounds us.

Particularly influential is the name we are given and its meaning. In addition to our given name, the label we are identified by in the family unit–being referred to as the clown, hero, care-taker, or the black sheep–has a lasting effect and is deeply resistant to change. These labels often exert a major influence over our life choices for many years and they help form the lens through which we see ourselves. The power of these labels is one of the reasons people sometimes experience discomfort at family reunions or funerals. Regardless of how we may have grown or changed over the years, when we are reunited with people who have been an important part of our lives they often continue to reflect back to us who we once were but not who we are now.

Sometimes these early family experiences can help set the stage for a life that is rich and meaningful, and at other times, like for my friend Phoebe, they can set the course for rough waters.

Upon Further Reflection

I'm embarrassed to admit it, but the thing I remember most about my first meeting with Phoebe was the smell. That and her disheveled, nearly blue hair.

She lived in a cramped little mobile home with three cats and a mangy old dog. Upon entering her space, the smell hit me in the face like a pungent pile driver. Instantly I knew this was going to be a breathe-through-the-mouth visit and made a mental note to pick up some Vicks Vaporub to keep in the car for future visits. (Over the years I've learned a little smear of the gel in each nostril is useful for such situations.)

After my usual introduction Phoebe let me know straight away she didn't want to talk about dying. Her daughter was getting married in a few months and Phoebe was going to walk her daughter down the aisle–death be damned.

Over the months my admiration for Phoebe's strength and courage grew exponentially. As we got to know each other she shared how, when she was growing up, her father had been an alcoholic who worked in the oil fields and would be gone for months at a time. Her mother suffered from some sort of mental disease and was abusive. For example, if young Phoebe misbehaved, her mother would take scissors, cut Phoebe's hair in an ugly fashion, and lock her in a closet for hours at a time.

She finally broke free from her mother as a young teenager and ran off with an abusive man who gave her a pager. When the man paged, Phoebe had to come home instantly to give him sexual gratification or he would burn her with cigarettes.

When she learned she was pregnant she found the courage to break free from him out of concern for her soon-to-be-born daughter. Then a miracle happened. Somehow she ended up going to a small church where she had a profound experience with the incredibly loving acceptance of God's grace.

That changed everything. Almost. Because of the way she had been raised, when Phoebe did things she thought were "bad," she would cut her own hair in an ugly fashion and then later try to super glue hair back onto her bald head. She told me for years she had to wear a wig to cover up her obsession. She also struggled with the tormenting fear that she would turn out to be just like her mother.

But somehow over the years–through the kindness of people in the small church and by the liberating grace of God–Phoebe had overcome it all. So, there was no way she was going to miss her daughter's wedding.

Of course, she did walk her daughter down the aisle, and with no wig but with her own beautiful disheveled hair. Shortly thereafter, her condition diminished to the point that Phoebe had to leave her small mobile home and move into a Skilled Nursing Home where she could receive the care she needed. This was very hard for her. Phoebe had had to fight just to survive for so much of her life. Surrendering just wasn't in her make-up.

On one of my last visits, Phoebe asked me why I had continued to come see her in her smelly little mobile home.

I told her because I had come to not only like her but to admire her.

"Admire *me*? For what?"

"Because you are an icon of hope for me. You have taught me that people can change–that I can change. You weren't condemned by the way you were brought up to turn out like your mom…you've been a great mother. You were able to break free from a horrible past by the power of love and grace. And that gives me hope."

She cried.

I cried.

That moment was saturated with a feeling I can only describe as holy.

In thinking about what made that moment so special I have come to believe it is simply because I was reflecting back to Phoebe a part of who she was that she had forgotten. That moment helped ease her suffering for a while. Phoebe became a good friend and a great teacher. She taught me the power of positive reflection.

The Shaping of Our Worldview

In addition to our nuclear family, another powerful reflection we assimilate into the work of crafting our meta-narrative of who we are and why we are comes from our culture. Cultural messages and mores act as powerful lenses through which we comprehend reality. These often-unseen elements exert incredible influence over the ways in which we experience and interpret reality.

In one of the more popular TED Talks, Ed Pariser describes what he calls "filter bubbles." He points out how Google, Yahoo, and other search engines all utilize filter bubbles to try and intuit what the searcher is actually looking for when she or he types in a topic to be searched. All of the internet search engines track the most frequently visited websites by each customer and then create, via an algorithm of filters, returned data from a search query. Pariser argues that, while this may serve advertisers paying the search engines, it limits our freedom to learn. These engines are simply reflecting back to us what we already know and have interest in. This example is simply a microcosm of what our culture does for and to us. Culture is a master filter of how we interpret reality.

Let's take a brief look into four components I deem essential to crafting our understanding of reality. In no particular order, they are: geography, social habitus, mythology, and ethics.

Geography

The actual physical space in which we live is a major contributor to our self-understanding. This idea is underscored by the often-quoted line of Jose Ortega y Gasset: "Tell me the landscape in which you live and I will tell you who you are" (Lane 2002, p.20). The physical terrain (i.e. mountains, plains, ocean, and desert) and climate (hot, cold, rainy, and dry) where we dwell play a significant role in our choice of careers, and, as I have argued, our life role is a major factor in our experience of meaning. In a very real way the natural geography of where we live reflects back to us who we are in this world and how to be in this world.

The importance of geography upon our self-understanding has been highlighted by the research of folks like Oscar Handlin, describing the archetypal experiences of Eastern European immigrants on American soil in the late 19th century:

> "I was born in such a village in such a parish"–so the peasant invariably began the account of himself. Thereby he indicated the importance of the village in his being; this was the fixed point by which he knew his position in the world and his relationship with all humanity. Human existence is heavily dependent upon such fixed points; they enable one to "dwell" in the world with meaning. (Lane 2002, p.34)

What Handlin and others have discovered is that our literal roots–where we come from geographically–help shape our self-understanding and view of the world in very profound and often unseen ways.

To go one step further, in his *Landscapes of the Sacred: Geography and Narrative in American Spirituality*, Belden Lane asserts that the natural environment we live in helps shape our souls and our souls help shape the artificial environments we create. "Who we are, in other words, is inseparably a part of where we are" (Lane 2002, p.6).

Social Habitus

Our worldview is not only shaped by our physical space, but by our social space as well. The instinctual search for tribal identity we need to create our life story has been identified and studied cogently by, among others, Pierre Bourdieu. He describes this very human activity as *habitus* (Bourdieu 1989). It is that drive within us to identify ourselves as Democrats or Republicans, Dodger or Yankee fans, lovers of opera or country music, and members of ACLU (the American Civil Liberties Union) or the NRA (the National Rifle Association). We actively seek out others who are like-minded and will reflect back to us the "we" we want to be or want to become.

For Bourdieu, "habitus are the generative and unifying principles with which we interpret our life" (1996, p.15). These "affinities of habitus" form the basis for whom we love and whom we hate, who our friends are and who our enemies are, and they even help determine whom we will marry or partner with–they have power over all of our relationships.

This project of creating a social space is not only an individual enterprise but a collective one as well. Habitus not only help define our sense of place but also the sense of place of others. For Bourdieu, the essential point is that these social categories become real and symbolic differences and create a very real language of their own: "The social space is indeed the first and last reality" (1996, p.22).

Mythology

In his classic text *The Hero with a Thousand Faces* (2008), Joseph Campbell explains that cultural myths help encode for a society what is and what is not acceptable behavior by its members. They are deeply held narratives about what is important for the life of the individual and the community and what constitutes right from wrong.

Working in an often invisible way, myths act as an interpretive lens through which we make mundane and important life decisions. They are the scaffolding to what we aspire to be. They help us define our place, our role in society. But as Campbell warns, if we disregard the cultural myth, we will be "broken-off" and become "simply nothing–waste" (2008, p.331).

For example, one of our foundational American myths centers on the idea of individualism. Innumerable movie scripts, songs, and novels portray the hero bucking a whole system to declare his or her independence. From John Wayne to Rambo, from the early pioneers to modern-day self-made millionaires, we Americans highly value the rights of the individual, often over those of the community at large.

Now, this mythological ethos of individualism has significant consequences on our end-of-life care and the numerous ethical issues involved with this care. This becomes our next field of cultural examination.

Ethics

The import of the American mythological ideal of individualism has significant ramifications on our ideas about the delivery of healthcare. Ethics are the ideals we utilize in order to live in harmony with one another and are aids in arriving at the best possible solution for difficult situations. Simply put, ethics help us determine what is right and what is wrong. In the world of American healthcare today, the ethic that trumps all others is a patient's *autonomy*.

The English word "autonomy" is derived from combining two Greek words that essentially mean self-rule. This approach, a direct consequence of our cultural mythological ideal of individualism, has greatly contributed to the current ethical crisis in end-of-life issues. Men and women are now making choices for themselves that heretofore only God could legitimately make: when and how human life comes to an end. With the advent of cardiopulmonary resuscitation (CPR), ventilators, dialysis, organ transplants, feeding tubes, and the proliferation of antibiotics, we have turned the process of dying into a nightmare. We are the very first generation of human beings on the planet who have ever had to contend with the ethical dilemmas created by these modern medical interventions, and we are often at a loss on how to do so.

Now all of this may strike you as simply theoretical, but I deal with the practical implications of this interplay between social space, mythology, and ethics on a daily basis. Possibly the best example of this existential distress for the dying I serve is captured by the experience of "feeling like a burden" to others. Remember, as Joseph Campbell warned, if we disregard the cultural myth we will be "broken-off" and become "simply nothing–waste." So many of the patients I visit are terrified of losing their autonomy, violating our national myth of independence, and creating hardship for the loved ones in their social space. They experientially feel like "a nothing, a waste," and this pain is one of the main reasons why folks here in Oregon opt for Physician Assisted Death. But this pain is essentially the result of our own mental constructs of reality based on our cultural worldview.

So, What's Your Story?

There is an African proverb that states, "We are made, not merely of flesh and blood, but of stories. Because that is what people are left with when we die–stories we told, stories others told about us, stories of our lives."[1] This wise saying captures the great project of being human. It highlights our need to craft a story of our lives, imbuing our time on this planet with some sort of meaning. The elements we draw from to create our stories come from our lived experiences, our nuclear family roles, our chosen tribe of relationships, and our concept of the Divine. This woven-together meta-narrative establishes the basis of our basic worldview–our life orientation.

Creating a meta-narrative for the meaning of our lives is much like printing a photograph by the old color-separation process. In order to print a color picture, the photograph had to be separated into four different-colored sheets of acetate: cyan, magenta, yellow, and black. Looking at each sheet separately, a person could see only a partial view

---

1   This proverb was shared with the author in a personal conversation with Fr. Freddy Ocun at St. Vincent Hospital in Portland, OR, on July 20, 2016.

of the picture. There were many blanks and missing pieces. Only when the four sheets were stacked on top of each other did the whole picture become clear. The combination of those four separate sheets made possible an infinite variety of color for the finished piece. So, instead of four different-colored acetates, we pull together our personal lived experiences, bits reflected to us from the people in our lives, pieces from our culture, and our personal transcendental beliefs (our God concept, which we'll explore in the next chapter) to portray our life story–all for the purpose of making sense out of our experiences and existence.

The stories we weave together from these various strands of information create our basic *orientation* to life and to the way things ought to be. These stories are very fragile and at some point will be assaulted. Throughout our lives, we experience unexpected and often tragic events. This *disorientation* requires that we reconfigure our meta-narratives. The great 20th-century rabbi Abraham Heschel observed that often our most valuable reflective insights occur as a result of our dramatic failures (Heschel 1965). This liminal space of disorientation is pregnant with opportunity to experience a radical *reorientation*–an opportunity for expansive spiritual growth, or conversely a deep soul wound. How we craft the story makes all the difference.

Orientation, disorientation, and reorientation[2]–this process plays out over and over again in the course of our lives and becomes the interpretive lens through which we evaluate who we are and what our life means in this mysterious expansive universe.

There is one more ingredient we use to craft our foundational life story, which we'll explore in the next chapter, and that is our concept of the Sacred.

---

2   This tripartite schema (orientation, disorientation, reorientation) has been identified and explored by Walter Brueggemann (*Spirituality of the Psalms*), by Joseph Campbell (*The Hero with a Thousand Faces*), and by Aristotle (*Poetics*).

6

Connecting with the Sacred

When I first met Erika, she was lying on her bed, talked nearly non-stop for an hour, and was easily tearful. She lived in a small apartment that was crammed to overflowing with stuff. There were books and knick-knacks everywhere and trails through the maze of bric-a-brac for her little white yappy dog to explore.

Erika was a Theosophist (a semi-religious practice begun in New York City during the late 19th century). Theosophists attempted to distill wisdom from various ancient religions, science, and philosophy into a comprehensive life practice. Their motto was "There is no religion higher than truth." A major teacher of this life practice was a man named Djwal Khul, whose writings (after his demise) were claimed to have been telepathically transmitted to his secretary Alice Bailey. There is great speculation as to who really authored the ideas of Theosophism, Djwal or Alice.

In addition to Theosophism, Erika had also explored the writings of Rudolph Steiner, an Anthroposophist (a little more spiritually mystical than Theosophists), who started the Waldorf schools. Erika shared stories about traveling to Europe in her 20s and, while in Paris, realized she had been there before "in another life" and had walked down the Champs-Élysées to a guillotine. She told me she hoped she was ready for "the great adventure" (as her teacher Djwal Khul referred to death). During her monologue, Erika wept several times as she explained to me that she was emotionally very sensitive.

Living with Erika in her stuffed little apartment was her daughter Jasmine, who waited dutifully on Erika's every whim. Erika also had another daughter (18 years older than Jasmine) who lived in upstate Oregon and ran a cannabis dispensary. Erika and this other daughter had been estranged for many years.

Now, I had heard from Erika's nurse that Erika and Jasmine did not get along well either. It seems Jasmine felt deep resentment for all of the time, attention, and money Erika had invested in her own spiritual pursuits, thus neglecting her role as mother. In fact, Jasmine ended up mothering Erika for most of their lives.

The day before my last visit to Erika, her nurse told me that Erika and Jasmine had a wonderful reconciliation and Jasmine had come to understand on a new level her mother's deep need for acceptance. It was a profoundly grace-filled experience for both of them.

When I arrived the next day, Erika was nearing death, and I asked her if she felt there was anything she needed to do before she died. She replied, "Let's get quiet for five or ten minutes and see what surfaces." So we sat quietly for ten minutes or so. Erika held my hand during this time. After the quiet, Erika asked me, "Is there anything else I need to do?"

I replied, "I don't think so...you've been a seeker your whole life... you've devoted yourself to your spiritual development...you've done well." Erika visibly relaxed and thanked me. I also reminded her about the loving exchange she had with Jasmine the day before as evidence of her spiritual work. We talked about the miracle of love, grace, forgiveness, and acceptance...the more you give them away, the more you get. For the first time in my two visits, Erika looked peaceful.

I remember another hospice patient named Bert. He told me for years he had attended an Episcopalian church but was very frustrated because the rector never really addressed Bert's desire to get "saved." Bert said that many times he had prayed "the sinner's prayer" as advertised on TV but never really felt saved. He was hoping I could help him have the authentic salvific experience. *Saved*, of course, is a religious code word for being accepted by God. Bert shared, "My biggest fear is not being in God's will."

Erika and Bert were two spiritual seekers from two very different faith traditions, both aching for the same thing–acceptance. This acceptance stuff is a big deal. We all are driven by it–sometimes to extremes. Some of the most devout patients I have encountered are terrorized by the idea they have not done enough to please God. Their God concepts were a source of fear and punishment, and profoundly shaped their worldviews.

This is contrasted by a passage from theologian Karl Rahner, who spoke about "the totality of humanity which God will never allow to escape from his love" (Rahner and Griffiths 1980, p.26). Another spiritual seeker with a very different worldview.

So, the question is, how is your God concept shaping your worldview?

What Is Your Concept of God?

Years ago, while on a trip to Israel, I was sitting on a boat on the Sea of Galilee. It was a beautiful sunny day. People were eating box lunches, the tour guide was yammering away about something, and I was simply daydreaming. I began to think of all the time and money and energy human beings for eons have put into erecting temples, creating rituals, and writing sacred texts–all in an effort to connect with the transcendent. Unfathomable hours of time, innumerable amounts of gold and silver, unexplainable ecstatic experiences. Something deep in our wiring reaches outward to the great Unknown. Rabbi Heschel puts it like this: "Being human involves being sensitive to the sacred. The objects regarded as sacred may differ from country to country, yet sensitivity to the sacred is universal" (1965, p.48). Amen.

Therefore, the final element to explore in the work we do to create our life story involves our concept of the Divine. Centuries ago John Calvin posited that "without knowledge of self there is no knowledge of God... and without knowledge of God there is no knowledge of self" (Kunkel et al. 1999, p.193). Whatever our beliefs about transcendence, they play a crucial role in our understanding of ourselves and our place in the universe (Gorsuch and Wong-McDonald 2004). Our search for meaning, community, and self are transformed when they are imbued with a sacred dimension.

Conversely, for many Christians the great religious existential fear is, as my patient Bert put it, "not being in God's will." This sentiment really touches upon the four great existential fears identified by Dr. Yalom that were discussed in Chapter 1; if there is a God then we are not *alone*, our *freedom* is meant as a test to obey God, *meaning* is found in doing God's will, and *death* is a doorway to our reward or judgment for how well we did. So many devout believers I have met struggled with thoughts like "God must still have something more for me to do." This is the God concept at work.

A metaphor might be helpful at this point. On your computer there is an operating system (either Windows or Apple) that enables all of your software programs to function properly. Now this operating system works invisibly in the background. Our God concept is like that, it invisibly works in the background of our reasoning, but it influences all of the decisions we make.

I use the terms "God concept," "Divine," and "transcendence" interchangeably, and I simply mean the way in which we understand our connection with that Something larger than ourselves. Our God concept may be informed by sacred texts like the Bible or the Qu'ran, or by beliefs in such things as astrology, philosophy, and paranormal experiences. Wherever we draw our beliefs about the transcendent from, researchers have identified 11 primary God concepts that affect our self-understanding: "Benevolent, Wrathful, Omni, Guiding, False, Stable, Deistic, Worthless, Powerful, Condemning, and Caring" (Wong 2012, p.175). Now this goes far beyond mere religion. Recent studies have shown that people with a positive God image (regardless of any particular faith or sect) are more self-directed, cooperative, and securely attached, while those with a fearful God concept are more likely to exhibit psychological distress.

Current findings reveal that a believer selects a "god" that is consistent with their own self-image (Benson and Spilka 1973). It seems Merton was right after all when he wrote, "Our idea of God tells us more about ourselves than Him" (Merton 2003, p.17).

In exploring how our God concept informs our experience and understanding of healing and end-of-life issues, I look to the wisdom of theologian Martin Marty and his brilliant essay "Religion and healing: the four expectations" (1988). Marty's aim was to address how people actually integrate their faith with their healing process. Rather than expressing the 11 primary God concepts listed above, Marty distills the connections between faith and healing down to four: autogenesis, synergism, monergism, and empathy.

He describes the autogenetic perspective by the slogan "I am master of my own fate" (Marty 1988, p.64). This approach places great importance on the choices one makes to live a healthy lifestyle and on preventative care. The synergistic viewpoint is expressed by the phrase "I am in tune with the infinite" (p.67). Folks with this belief system are open to holistic healthcare which allows for the merging of Western and Eastern therapeutic ideas and their connections with the spirit. "God worked a miracle in me" (p.76) is the cry of the monergist. The emphasis here is that one is healed by the direct intervention of the one and only true God. Finally, the empathic person feels, "God experiences with me" (p.70). Adherents with this God concept work to fuse their faith with the wisdom of scientific Western medicine. Marty makes clear these four positions are not clear cut, absolute, or confined to particular faith traditions or denominations, and concedes there are overlaps. All in all, I find his observations very helpful in understanding how a person's God concept informs the lives of the patients I serve and give me clues on how best to communicate with them.

A final aspect of our God concept I'd like to address is that, unlike the Ten Commandments, it is not static or fixed in stone. As we experience life's traumas and joys, as we gather new information, we reformulate our understanding of the Divine. My own understanding of God has certainly evolved over the years. My heartfelt prayer is that I continually grow to discover the Real God and allow my illusionary self-imagined god images to fall away.

The Crying God

A number of years ago we lived in England, and I was on the leadership team of a small network of independent churches. I remember one dramatic event in particular. There was a horrible train wreck at Paddington Station. A commuter train crashed, killing 30 people. A number of them were from one of our congregations in Reading. That Sunday, at church, several people stood to give thanks to God for sparing their loved ones. One person said, "My husband was sick that day, or he would have been on that train." The congregation clapped in joyous approval, and gave thanks to God. As I sat there, I thought about others in the congregation who had lost loved ones. Didn't God care about them?

Now this brings up the whole question about what theologians call *theodicy*. While this is neither the time nor place to discuss this topic (libraries of books are written on this theme with no consensus of thought or comforting resolution), theologian Frederick Buechner states the problem succinctly:

- God is all-powerful.

- God is all-good.

- Terrible things happen.

You can reconcile any two of these propositions with each other, but you can't reconcile all three. The problem of evil is perhaps the greatest single problem for religious faith (2016, p.64).

While Buechner does not offer any concrete solution to this dilemma, he does offer sage advice: "All-wise. All-powerful. All-loving. All-knowing. We bore to death both God and ourselves with our chatter. God cannot be expressed, only experienced" (2016, p.69).

A recent conversation. We had a patient on our hospice service who was a beautiful loving elderly man of deep faith. His wife had died the week before, and he was in tormenting pain due to tumors pressing on the nerves around his spine. Bedbound, tortured, and longing for death. One of my chaplain colleagues lamented, "Why won't God just take him?"

My response: "Is that what you think? That God kills people? Because if we say God comes to take him, then God must also come and take the children from the pediatric cancer wards and the infants from their mother's arms in the NICU."

My chaplain friend hedged her bet and suggested, "Well, what I mean is that God *calls* us home."

"Then don't answer the phone!" was my irreverent reply.

I know what she was trying to convey. I've read all of the same theological arguments. "We use words like omniscient, omnipotent, omnipresent, and sovereignty like we know what they mean" (Wiman 2013, p.18). Words to construct an idea of the Divine Other we name God to make us feel safe and right. Then we kill each other trying to defend these words when they simply unravel in the cold heart light of reality.

"So what do *you* think?" she curtly shot back.

"I think when we die, God cries. I think God cries over the missed opportunities we had to give and receive love because we were too afraid–afraid we were not worthy of love. I think God cries over the cruelty we unleash on each other out of the fear of not having enough. I think God cries over our not knowing how God aches for communion with us."

My friend turned away exasperated by me and my questions. I think that's a result of my spending too much time with Death–he's taught me to be wary of any god who stands by unmoved when we need Her most.

Dallas Willard says, "The acid test for *any* theology is this: is the God presented one that can be loved heart, soul, mind and strength?" (1998, p.329).

Think about It

Some number of years ago, while in the throes of a romantic union, your father discharged over 250 million spermatozoa into your mother's uterus which all scrambled in a life or death dash up her fallopian tubes to fertilize her one and only egg. Two hundred and fifty million. Talk about winning the lottery–you are a one in 250 million shot. That's nearly the whole population of the United States. And only one made it. You.

Once fertilized, this newly created zygote triggered a delicately balanced series of sequential genetic codes, trillions of them, beginning the process of developing your brain, heart, liver, kidneys, and skeletal structure. For nine gestating months this amazing process hummed along in the relative safety of your mother's uterus. The odds for something to have gone wrong are staggering.

Then one day you were unceremoniously pushed through a very tight elastic canal only to be greeted by a rather hard slap on your never-before-touched gluteus maximus. This action energized your developing lungs to produce the air flow necessary to emit your first sounds. Naked, alone, and completely vulnerable, you entered this reality.

Susceptible to untold gazillions of germs and bacteria, totally dependent upon others for warmth and nourishment, you begin this stage of your precarious journey we call life.

Learning from your nuclear family how to behave and communicate, you began to make choices which helped shape who you are today. Your language. Your interests. Your experiences. Your choice of friends. Of schools. Of lovers. All of these choices and innumerable more have contributed to the particular human being you are right here and now.

And where is here?

Somewhere on planet Earth I'll bet.

> Did you know that this rock we all live on is tilted at a 23 degree angle, and scientists tell us that if the earth was not tilted exactly like this vapors from the oceans moving both north and south would create continents of ice. If the moon were only 50,000 miles away from earth instead of 200,000, the tides might be so enormous that all continents would be submerged in water–even the mountains would be eroded... If the crust of the earth had been only ten feet thicker, there would be no oxygen... Had the oceans been a few feet deeper, carbon dioxide and oxygen would have been absorbed and no vegetable life would exist... The nine major planets in our solar system range in distance from the sun from 36 million to about 3 trillion, 6664 billion miles; yet each moves around the sun in exact precision... Still, the sun is only a minor star in the 100 billion orbs which comprise our Milky Way galaxy. If you were to hold a dime, a ten-cent piece, at arm's length, the coin would block out 15 million stars from your view, if your eyes could see with that power. (Manning 1990, pp.31-33)

Of most importance, of course, is when reflecting on the not-to-be fathomed number of atoms and choices that must align in exact precision for you to be you and for your experience of this life to be what it is, are you overwhelmed by gratitude? Can you weep from happiness and gratitude? Do you savor the beauty of the most simple act or common object? All of this begs the most important question, what are you going to do with this one miraculous gift of God–your life?

Whether you're like me and believe there is an intentionally loving initiator we name God behind all of these incalculable odds for life as we know it, or you believe that this experience of life is simply a random happenstance of the right molecules aligning together–both views require faith. And whatever God concept we put our faith in influences nearly every aspect of our lived experience. It impacts the kind of father I am, the kind of wife, citizen, friend, employee. It affects how I spend my money and my time. For example, do we see this planet's resources as simply ours for the taking to use any way we see fit for our own pleasure, or do we share a deep reverence for all of creation and see ourselves as stewards for future generations? The answer flows from our God concept. May "your concept of God be feisty and imaginative and rich enough to incorporate all the hungers of your heart" (O'Donohue 2012).

7

Connecting with Others
Part One—Forgiveness

An Archetypal Story

The serpent was clever, more clever than any wild animal God had made. He spoke to the Woman: "Do I understand that God told you not to eat from any tree in the garden?"

The Woman said to the serpent, "Not at all. We can eat from the trees in the garden. It's only about the tree in the middle of the garden that God said, 'Don't eat from it; don't even touch it or you'll die.'"

The serpent told the Woman, "You won't die. God knows that the moment you eat from that tree, you'll see what's really going on. You'll be just like God, knowing everything, ranging all the way from good to evil."

When the Woman saw that the tree looked like good eating and realized what she would get out of it–she'd know everything!–she took and ate the fruit and then gave some to her husband, and he ate.

Immediately the two of them did "see what's really going on"–saw themselves naked! They sewed fig leaves together as makeshift clothes for themselves.

When they heard the sound of God strolling in the garden in the evening breeze, the Man and his Wife hid in the trees of the garden, hid from God.

God called to the Man: "Where are you?"

He said, "I heard you in the garden and I was afraid because I was naked. And I hid."

God said, "Who told you you were naked? Did you eat from that tree I told you not to eat from?"

The Man said, "The Woman you gave me as a companion, she gave me fruit from the tree, and, yes, I ate it."

God said to the Woman, "What is this that you've done?"

"The serpent seduced me," she said, "and I ate."

God told the serpent:

> *"Because you've done this, you're cursed,*
> *cursed beyond all cattle and wild animals,*
> *Cursed to slink on your belly*
> *and eat dirt all your life.*
> *I'm declaring war between you and the Woman,*
> *between your offspring and hers.*
> *He'll wound your head,*
> *you'll wound his heel."*

He told the Woman:

> *"I'll multiply your pains in childbirth;*
> *you'll give birth to your babies in pain.*
> *You'll want to please your husband,*
> *but he'll lord it over you."*

He told the Man:

> *"Because you listened to your wife*
> *and ate from the tree*
> *That I commanded you not to eat from,*
> *'Don't eat from this tree,'*
> *The very ground is cursed because of you;*
> *getting food from the ground*
> *Will be as painful as having babies is for your wife;*
> *you'll be working in pain all your life long.*
> *The ground will sprout thorns and weeds,*
> *you'll get your food the hard way,*

Planting and tilling and harvesting,
sweating in the fields from dawn to dusk,
Until you return to that ground yourself, dead and buried;
you started out as dirt, you'll end up dirt."

The Man, known as Adam, named his wife Eve because she was the mother of all the living.

God made leather clothing for Adam and his wife and dressed them.

God said, "The Man has become like one of us, capable of knowing everything, ranging from good to evil. What if he now should reach out and take fruit from the Tree-of-Life and eat, and live forever? Never–this cannot happen!"

So God expelled them from the Garden of Eden and sent them to work the ground, the same dirt out of which they'd been made. He threw them out of the garden and stationed angel-cherubim and a revolving sword of fire east of it, guarding the path to the Tree-of-Life. (Genesis 3, The Message[1])

Now whether you believe this biblical story, often called *The Fall*, really took place or not, the diagnosis of our human condition offered by the sacred author is spot on. We have all at times felt our souls estranged from creation, God, others, and even ourselves.

For healing this disease of soul estrangement, the medicine of forgiveness is most effective. And forgiveness, like all powerful remedies, is tricky stuff. Before using you should read the warning label and consider the dosage. This is because the core ingredients of forgiveness are truth and honesty–which can kill as well as heal. If we use truth as a bludgeon to shame someone or extract revenge, the result will only perpetuate and magnify the estrangement. Truth and honesty can only be agents of liberation when applied within the context of restoring relationships–in a desire for reconciliation.

In one episode of NPR's *On Being*, the host Krista Tippett was interviewing former director of research for the South African Truth and Reconciliation Commission Charles Villa-Vicencio. If you remember, the Truth and Reconciliation Commission was instituted by Nelson Mandela

---

1   (2004) *NIV/The Message Parallel Bible*. Grand Rapids, MI: Zondervan, pp.4-6.

as a means of providing healing for South Africans after the oppressive years of *apartheid*. In that interview Villa-Vicencio shared these startling observations:

> Some people, especially in the early days of the Truth and Reconciliation Commission, somehow thought that what was being suggested is that if we all told the truth, we will all be reconciled. You know, simple as that. You do A, you'll have B, which is absolute nonsense. Let me put it to you this way, if I may, that if we want to talk about justice or we want to talk about truth outside of the desire to be reconciled, outside of the desire to build a relationship, outside of the desire to move on, if it's outside of that, then truth and justice can be a very destructive and a very vindictive thing. I think one of the fundamental philosophical roots of the Truth and Reconciliation is an African notion of *ubuntu*. Ubuntu loosely translated means "humanity." It means to live together. It is a concept that says, "I am through you and you are through me." It's only as we engage in truthful dialogue and in a quest for building a relationship that we can grow as individual people. So to the extent of I am estranged from you, I am less than human. It's a relationship that is required... I come away from the commission perhaps learning two things, and that is, one, that human beings in certain circumstances are capable of the most outrageously treacherous deeds... You know what else I learned is that even those perpetrators–and I've met some bad ones, of all kinds of political persuasions–when you sit down and you talk, they are human beings. (Tippett 2007)

Another icon of reconciliation, Martin Luther King, sharpens this insight:

> Through our scientific and technological genius, we have made of this world a neighborhood, and yet we have not had the ethical commitment to make of it a brotherhood. But somehow, and in some way, we have got to do this. We must all learn to live together as brothers or we will all perish together as fools. We are tied together in the single garment of destiny, caught in an inescapable network of mutuality. And whatever affects one directly affects all indirectly. For some strange reason I can never be what I ought to be until you are what you ought

to be. And you can never be what you ought to be until I am what I ought to be. This is the way God's universe is made; this is the way it is structured. (King, Carson and Holloran 1998, pp.207–208)

Now Villa-Vicencio and King are addressing the need for forgiveness to be applied within the context of restoring relationships on a global level– as a remedy for the soul wounds of a nation or a community. But the same imperative applies when considering forgiveness for the personal, one-on-one, level as was shown me by my friend Marilyn.

Free at Last

It was an early Saturday morning when Becky, the on-call nurse, phoned to say that Marilyn was actively dying and her husband Lou wanted me to come and pray for her.

An hour later when I arrived, Marilyn's more than six-foot-tall frail body was lying comfortably on a hospital bed in the living room. Lou and son Alvin were doing fine. As we drank coffee and ate homemade pie (graciously provided by a kind neighbor), we shared favorite Marilyn stories. Like the time in their younger years when she wanted new living room furniture. Lou didn't. So while he was off at work Marilyn burned all of their old furniture in the fireplace and Lou came home that night to an empty house. The next day they went out and got new furniture.

And then there was the time when Marilyn was a young girl on the family farm and somehow accidentally cut off one of her fingers. She loved to tell how she was able to compartmentalize the pain in her brain as her mother put the severed finger on ice and drove her to the hospital where the digit was surgically reattached...all without pain medication. Her beloved father, a deeply spiritual man, had taught her how to ignore pain and she adored him.

Larger than life. That was Marilyn.

As I sat and watched her 91-year-old body breathe sporadically, I realized how in younger years she must have been a real head-turner. Tall, lithe, and full of life.

I remembered on my first visit being captivated by her infectious Phyllis-Diller-like laugh. I remembered too how on that first visit she pointedly asked me how to get free from the emotional pain of hating deceased family members.

"You won't like my answer," I said.

"What?" she pressed.

"You have to forgive them."

"You're right... I don't like your answer."

I shared with her one of my favorite quotes: "Unforgiveness is a poison we drink hoping somebody else will die." But she wasn't interested.

Her soul pain persisted. Seems that was pain she just couldn't compartmentalize.

On a subsequent visit, after I had earned some trust, Marilyn shared the source of that deep soul pain–her mother's dying at an early age led to the remarriage of her idolized father to a fairy-tale-like evil step-mother. I forget a lot of the details now, but it had something to do with the new step-mom stealing family monies and her father's affection from Marilyn. She even sheepishly confided to me how once she urinated on the step-mother's grave. While physically relieving, that act did nothing for the emotional pain. Years of being ostracized from her home and father's love had cut very deep. Marilyn never spoke of her step-mother again.

So it was with some surprise that months later Marilyn called to see me between our regular visits. That wasn't like her. She had called because she had wanted to tell me in person that my advice had worked. She was so proud of herself and happy to share that she was finally free of her soul's pain. In her own way and in her own pace Marilyn had worked on successfully forgiving a long-deceased step-mother, only to discover that she was the prisoner set free. That forgiveness is powerful stuff.

So after the coffee, pie, and stories...Lou and Alvin and I gathered around Marilyn's hospital bed, joined hands, and prayed that our beloved Marilyn would go gently into that place where the Book promises "there is no more suffering or tears or crying...or *pain*."

The Place of Hot Burning Coals

Before we consider some thoughts on the actual process of forgiving, another biblical story adds an important insight.

There is a particular Greek word, *anthrakian*, that is used in the whole New Testament only twice. The first occurrence of this word is found in the 18th chapter of John's gospel: "It was cold, and the servants and officials stood around a fire (*anthrakian*) they had made to keep warm. Peter also was standing with them, warming himself" (John 18.18, NIV).

Anthrakian literally means a fire of hot burning coals. If you remember the story, it was here at the place of hot burning coals that Peter denied three times he even knew Jesus.

Earlier in the evening (at what we call the Last Supper) Peter had proclaimed that even if all the other followers of Jesus got afraid and ran away, he wouldn't. Jesus could count on him. Obviously Peter failed.

Jump ahead to the last chapter in John's story and we find the word *anthrakian* again. Jesus has risen from the dead and keeps appearing and disappearing in an unpredictable manner. Peter decides to go fishing. That's what he knew. He was a fisherman.

After a fruitless night on the lake, Jesus appears and suggests where all the fish are. After the huge catch they realize it is Jesus and head to him on shore. Jesus is waiting there for them with breakfast cooking on a fire of hot burning coals (*anthrakian*).

During breakfast Jesus asks Peter three times if Peter really does love him. Three times Peter had disavowed knowing Jesus. Three times now he will affirm his true love.

There is another play on Greek words in this episode. The Greeks had several words for our one word, love. The word *philein* means to love like a brother loves (hence the name Philadelphia literally means city of brotherly love). The word *agapan* means to love perfectly, purely.

Jesus asks Peter twice if Peter really *agapes* Him. Peter answers that he loves Jesus but uses the word *philein*. Peter doesn't claim to be more dependable than others this time. He says in essence, "Jesus, I don't love you perfectly but I really do love you like a brother."

For the third time Jesus asks, "Peter, do you really love me?" This time Jesus too uses the word *philein*: "Peter, do you really love me like a brother?" This time Peter is hurt. Peter answers, "Lord, You know everything. Now doggone it, you know I really do love you like a brother."

Jesus has brought Peter back to the place of hot burning coals. He has brought Peter back to this place not to hurt him but to heal him. Jesus brings Peter back to the place of his failure to liberate him so that he can fulfill his destiny as a revealer of God's tender mercy.

We can't pick the time and place when we will be brought back to our places of hot burning coals, our places of failure. We can trust, however, that God will. And that it will be done not to hurt us...but to heal us.

But How Do I Forgive?

In many years as a hospice chaplain I have seen firsthand the enormous pain unforgiveness wreaks at the end of life. Simply put, folks holding onto deep-seated resentments require a lot more analgesics (big-time pain killers) as they are dying. A lot more. And it never really seems to alleviate the suffering. I have come to learn that the ability to forgive, oneself and others, is one of the surest markers in dying a peaceful death.

So, how do we forgive what feels like the unforgivable?

While I do not presume to definitively answer this painfully soul-searching question, in over 40 years of ministry and praying with thousands of folks in search of giving and receiving forgiveness, I'll share with you some insights distilled from these deeply personal and emotional experiences.

The first thing to be acknowledged is that we can never truly know the depth of another person's soul injury (or quite possibly even our own for that matter). I remember praying one time with a young Black woman who said that her two great sources of pain were a husband who had cheated on her by sleeping with her best friend, and a memory of some middle school classmates teasing her because she was Black. Before praying, I assumed that forgiving the husband would be much more difficult. Wrong.

Another young woman shared how traumatic it had been for her when as a child after coming home from tonsillectomy surgery she had been brushing her teeth and saw blood. Believing she was bleeding to death, she ran to her mother for comfort and Mom just blew her off, saying,

"Here, help me finish the dishes." To me, this seemed a minor incident. Not so for the young woman.

So, because we can't measure the depth of pain for a soul injury, there is no one approach or prescription for forgiving. There are, however, some ingredients that can be applied to soothe and offer healing.

I have learned that forgiving ourselves and others is best done from a place of relative safety–both physically and emotionally. You can't rush it. If you are still in an emotionally raw place of hurt, you simply can't just "do the right thing" and grind your way through it. There are no bypasses on the road to authentic soul healing. The depth of forgiveness both given and received is often much more profound when we are in a secure and balanced state of mind. This means being physically safe, relatively free from economic stress, and emotionally supported by loved ones. From this solid soul ground the heroic task of forgiveness can best be initiated.

Another consideration is what some Buddhists refer to as "dependent origination" (Siegel 2014, p.120). This simply means that every event originates from causes and conditions. Considering the implications of this requires a more impersonal perspective. For example, if someone hurt you or withheld something from you, this perspective asks you to consider that the other person hurting you was wounded themselves. That possibly their action was the result of their deep woundedness, and not necessarily a personal attack on you? Often, people treat others as they treat themselves.

It is from this place, this broader, more impersonal, perspective that you can actually begin to forgive. Being emotionally connected to the pain, having a broader perspective of all that was going on at the time and the truthful conditions surrounding the event–here in this vulnerable moment being able to forgive and inviting God to forgive the other or yourself can be quite liberating. I have not only seen it with my own eyes. I have experienced it.

Within the Christian tradition there is a rich history of going to a priest or minister, a sister or a brother, or a trusted friend and doing this verbally. The biblical foundation for this kind of intervention is found in James 5.16: "Therefore confess your sins to each other and pray for each other so that you may be healed" (NIV). I know from experience that there is something incredibly liberating in having another human being hear what is most shameful or painful in my life, praying with me, and then telling me I am forgiven. This is sacramental ministry.

Depending on how deep the wound is, this kind of practice may take a period of time and go through several stages. But the emotional intensity should decrease during each session. Also, you might consider asking for professional guidance if this kind of prayer and reflection becomes emotionally overwhelming. Some places are just too scary to go alone.

How do you know when forgiveness is complete? Many people feel a sense of peace and freedom, like an emotional boil has been lanced. But whether you feel anything in the moment or not, you know if you see the other person's name who was involved in the event, or hear their voice, or see their picture, or see the place where it took place–and none of the old emotions of shame and fear arise–that you are on the path of healing.

Several final words. Forgiveness is about getting free, it is not about forgetting. Having done the kind of things I have suggested, it would not be wise or skillful to place yourself back into a harmful situation or relationship. You will still remember what happened; it just won't hurt so deeply anymore.

I have a scar on my left index finger. When I was in college studying theater, I had a class in scenery building. One day I was cutting some wood with a power saw just as an attractive young actress walked by in a tight leotard. Distracted by the sight, I pulled the saw across my finger. Part of my finger was gone, blood spurting out, not a great way to meet girls I discovered. Years later I still have a scar, I remember the event, but there is no pain now. Forgiveness isn't about forgetting–it's about getting free from the pain.

Finally, I can say with a certain degree of certainty that most often the hardest person we end up having to forgive is ourselves. It is one thing to believe that God forgives us–it is quite another to actually forgive ourselves. It is only when we have truly forgiven ourselves that we will be at peace. Forgiving ourselves is in fact the actualization of the stated belief God has forgiven us.

A friend of mine used to say, "Hurt people hurt people. Free people free people." May you be the latter.

For Further Reflection

Here is a traditional Jewish prayer of confession used in preparation for
Yom Kippur (the Day of Atonement) and as one is approaching death:

> In the spirit and tradition of my fathers and mothers, I offer
> this prayer.
>
> Please forgive me for that which I need forgiveness for,
> for that which may still be heavy on my heart. Forgive me for
> the ways that I have missed the mark throughout my lifetime.
> Forgive me for the times that I have caused others pain. I did
> the best I could.
>
> And please forgive those who caused me pain. Forgive
> those who hurt me intentionally or unintentionally. May there
> be forgiveness and release.
>
> May it be possible now to experience a full healing: an
> opening, an allowing, a great compassion for myself and for
> others.
>
> I acknowledge before my ancestors and the great mystery I
> stand before, that my life and death are out of my hands. May
> I be sheltered in the shadow of great wings. May I be protected
> and guarded on this next journey, as I have been protected and
> guarded on the journeys that have brought me to this point.
>
> Protect my dear loved ones, with whose souls my soul is
> bound.[2]
>
> *Shema Israel Adonai Eloheinu Adonai Echad*
> *Hear O Israel, the Lord our God, the Lord is One.*

---

2   This translation of the Vidui is provided by my friend Rabbi Joshua Boettiger who
wrote it in honor of his grandmother, Posy Adler, and is used here with permission.

8

Connecting with Others
Part Two—Blessing

There is a Buddhist saying that goes, "When you are ready, your teacher will come." It took me nearly 64 years to get ready for Hattie.

Barely five-foot tall, 94 years young, Hattie was a force of nature. My friends Linda and Cyndi had been telling me about her for months before we actually met. And I confess I was a little nervous about meeting her. It's not because she was a famous artist, but more because my friends were so captivated by her and they were *really* sure Hattie and I would become dear friends. I don't do well under pressure.

Linda and her husband Ward had bought one of Hattie's paintings, then somehow they became friends and Hattie offered to give Linda painting lessons. Soon Linda invited Cyndi to join them. And after several months I got dragged up to the studio, not to paint, just to be enthralled.

Hattie was a connoisseur of classical music, astronomy, politics, UFOs, botany, art, and life. An incurable spiritual seeker, she referred to the One we name God as *Spook*. It was her endearing name for the Creator. Her interests were unbounded; she thrived on learning, didn't take herself or anyone else too seriously, and had a very dry and biting sense of humor. You could spend two hours talking with Hattie and it felt like five minutes.

But what I remember most about Hattie was her natural ability to bless nearly everyone she met. She could see deep into your soul, recognize your unspoken hopes and dreams, and call them forth into reality. She did that for my friends Linda and Cyndi who both had always aspired to be artists. She gave them paints, and canvasses, and lessons, and encouragement, and the freedom to become. And she helped me grow as a writer.

After being diagnosed with cancer, Hattie let me see a side of her she rarely revealed. It seems, a good number of years prior, Hattie had a gall bladder surgery that went amiss. The result left her incontinent of bowel. Every outing she took for decades was predicated on the availability of a suitable bathroom. Now this development not only cut her budding teaching career short (she had been hoping to take a position as chair of a prestigious art department), it also carried a large degree of embarrassment.

As she shared this very personal and painful part of her life story, we explored how this result of her surgery also had an unexpected fortunate outcome. Being restricted to her home for so much of her life enabled her to develop unique skills and produce a vast amount of widely sought-after art. She offhandedly commented, "If I'd have taken that department chair position I would never have become the artist I am today... I'd probably have become some sort of self-important know-it-all... Lucky me."

Hattie's ability to reframe difficult life lessons was a direct result of her intimate relationship with Spook. It was also the source of her innate ability to bless those who came into her circle of experience. "Spook loves me like I'm an only child," she would often say, "and the amazing thing is that Spook does that for everyone! I've learned it's my responsibility to make everyone in my life feel special like that."

A responsibility she faithfully carried out until her death. She endured the long, drawn-out dying process with the same generosity of spirit that animated so much of her living. For over six months as her abilities slowly declined, she would often say, "I'm ready to go...*what's Spook waiting for?*" But those months were such a blessing for those of us who loved her. They allowed so many of us odd souls Hattie had collected over the years to come and reflect back to her how significant Spook's grace that came through her had meant to each of us. It was an opportunity to give thanks for the gift of Hattie.

She was not only a famous painter, Hattie was an accomplished artist of life. Perhaps her greatest legacy is the beauty she called into existence from everyone who was ever blessed to call her their friend.

What Is a Blessing?

The previous chapters dealing with reflecting on our soul's wisdom, our story, our experience of God, and attending to our woundedness by way of forgiveness have all been designed to help us and those we serve unearth our soul's treasures–our authentic voices. Connecting with those things we most believe to be true and good. Once discovered, we can then share these uniquely remarkable gifts with those we love, as my friend Hattie did. That is now the focus of this chapter. We turn from inward reflection to outward blessing.

I am convinced the best way we can help senior adults prepare for a good death is by helping them live a fully engaged life now. I could cite more famous philosophers and spiritual teachers of all persuasions to reinforce my proposition–but I trust you've read them as well. The real question here is what can we do, as clergy and chaplains, to help facilitate this worthy goal. The primary way, I believe, is by working to strengthen the roles and relationships of those we serve.

And as people of religion one of the great and underutilized tools for relationship building in our arsenal is the *blessing*.

So, what exactly is a blessing? John O'Donohue, in his poetically Irish way, says:

> A blessing is different from a greeting, a hug, a salute, or an affirmation; it opens a different door in human encounter. One enters into the forecourt of the soul, the source of intimacy and the compass of destiny. (2008, p.199)

Several words in this idea from O'Donohue are significant for understanding a blessing and deserve further exploration. They are: human encounter, intimacy, soul, and destiny.

One of the sources of power contained in a blessing is that it builds on some type of human relationship. As will be seen, it is almost impossible to bless someone you know nothing about. So, relationship–human connection–is key. Now this need not be a longstanding relationship, but some depth of personal knowledge between the blesser and blessee is important.

In fact, a blessing is an invitation to greater intimacy in the relationship. When you bless someone, you are acknowledging that you see something of beauty within them and you are calling it forth to be actualized in reality. As I've shared, it's like the feeling Jake Sully had in the movie *Avatar* when Neytiri so powerfully said, "I see you." This kind of seeing takes the relationship to a whole new level.

This kind of seeing, of perceiving, is not done with the physical eyes, but rather with the eyes of your soul. O'Donohue again: "When you bless another, you first gather yourself; you reach below your surface mind and personality, down to the deeper source within you–namely, the soul" (2008, p.205). Blessings are not given off the cuff. They require reflection and thought. To prepare to give a blessing demands you spend time thinking about the person you want to bless, what attributes in them you see as beautiful, and then planning how to impart this observation in a soulful way.

And a true blessing speaks to the destiny of the one being blessed. "Blessing has pure agency, because it animates on the deepest threshold between being and becoming; it mines the territories of memory to awaken and draw forth possibilities we cannot even begin to imagine!" (O'Donohue 2008, p.217). Now, to have transformative power, a blessing must be rooted in what is already authentically resident in the other. It cannot be fabricated. You can't just make something up that sounds pretty for a blessing. If what you are calling forth from the one you are blessing isn't there already in embryonic form, the blessing will not connect–it has nothing to hold on to.

So, let me offer a working definition of what a blessing is for our soul legacy purposes: *a blessing is simply calling attention to a particularly special characteristic or quality in someone you love and encouraging that trait into greater realization.* Additionally, embedded within a blessing is the transformative power to heal old wounds, reframe past failures, and complete what is yet undone in our lives. Lessons gleaned from another archetypal biblical story.

Wrestling with God Knows What

That night Jacob got up and took his two wives, his two female servants and his eleven sons and crossed the ford of the Jabbok. After he had sent them across the stream, he sent over all his possessions. So Jacob was left alone, and a man wrestled with him till daybreak. When the man saw that he could not overpower him, he touched the socket of Jacob's hip so that his hip was wrenched as he wrestled with the man. Then the man said, "Let me go, for it is daybreak."

But Jacob replied, "I will not let you go unless you bless me."

The man asked him, "What is your name?"

"Jacob," he answered.

Then the man said, "Your name will no longer be Jacob, but Israel, because you have struggled with God and with humans and have overcome."

Jacob said, "Please tell me your name."

But he replied, "Why do you ask my name?" Then he blessed him there.

So Jacob called the place Peniel, saying, "It is because I saw God face to face, and yet my life was spared."

The sun rose above him as he passed Peniel, and he was limping because of his hip. Therefore to this day the Israelites do not eat the tendon attached to the socket of the hip, because the socket of Jacob's hip was touched near the tendon. (Genesis 32.22-32, NIV)

My reading of this mysterious Divine encounter is colored by what I know of the story's context. For example, there's the birth of Jacob and the significance of his name. Jacob was the second-born twin and, as the narrative goes, when his brother Esau first emerged from their mother's womb Jacob tried to pull him back in so that Jacob could be the firstborn. Being firstborn in that time and place was very important. The firstborn son got twice as much of an inheritance as each of the other sons (the birthright), as well as the right to become patriarch of the clan when the current patriarch died.

Names were also very important in that culture. They were not given arbitrarily but spoke to the character and nature of the one named. Because Jacob grabbed his brother's heel as he was being born, he was given the name Jacob, which literally meant "surplanter" or, in our vernacular, "little thief."

And a thief he was. In the ensuing years, Jacob not only conned Esau out of his birthright, but he even stole their father's blessing. Rabbi Marc Gafni notes, "Each child is granted his own blessing, reflecting his unique destiny. When Jacob stole Esau's blessing, he stole his brother's soul"

(2001, p.81). This so infuriated his older brother that Jacob had to escape to their uncle Laban for safety. Even there, Jacob's character got him into trouble. Jacob conned Laban (a shifty man himself) out of livestock and had to flee for his life.

Jacob had ripped off his brother and uncle and had to flee two homes. Now word came that Esau was advancing to meet Jacob with an army of 400 men. His life of stealing from others had caught up with him. Jacob was frightened and alone. Alone in his existential distress to gaze into the abyss of who he really was and the harm he had caused others.

That's the back story to our biblical episode. Now it is the night before the big meeting with Esau and the biblical author tells us that a man, an angel, or God (the sacred writer seems to be as mystified as we are) appears–and, what's even more startling, *attacks* Jacob. In fact, they fight all night.

As dawn begins to break, an amazing thing takes place. The Stranger blesses Jacob. This blessing results in a name change, signifying the deep character transformation that has taken place as a result of this Divine encounter. No longer "little thief," Jacob is now Israel, "one who wrestles with God." And what is the sign that he has been spiritually transformed? He walks with a limp.

Whatever else is happening in this story it is clear that God's blessing transforms Jacob's character, heals old wounds, reframes past failures, and is the foundation for Jacob/Israel's future destiny and that of his whole family. That was one powerful blessing.

Blessings have the potential to help shape the destiny of the one blessed.

As the Genesis story moves forward Jacob does have a peaceful reconciliation with Esau and Jacob takes his place in Israel's patriarchy. In fact, the concluding two chapters of this first biblical book recount the detailed blessings Jacob, now Israel, gives to each of his sons. Because he has received a blessing he can now give blessings.

I remember clearly waking up one morning after a weekend of bingeing on my favorite forms of self-soothing (wrestling with my own God knows what), and the thought that surfaced from my numbed soul was: "You're just a frightened little boy aching to belong." Now as crazy as this may sound, this realization wasn't condemning but rather liberating.

I grasped on a deep level that we all feel this way. We all struggle with the existential fear of being alone and long for real connection with others.

But our attempts to connect are often misguided and only lead to greater isolation. Consider our addictions to social media. We check in with these electronic pseudo-connections so many times throughout the day because our souls are starving for real touch. Most of the things posted on Facebook are simply the projections our false self[1] wants the world to see, like those supercilious Christmas newsletters that tout all of our wonderful achievements over the past year. Pure nonsense. In this inauthentic digital universe our false self is futilely attempting to connect with and control the type of relationship we have with the false selves of people we know–and our soul remains starved for real belonging. Real relationships cannot be controlled, they must be wild and free if they are to be life giving.

This dearth of reality actually increases our soul's hunger for authentic belonging. And herein lays the transformative power of a genuine blessing. When someone blesses us, they look past the projected image of our false self and unearth a treasure resident in our authentic self. They lovingly and thoughtfully perceive a graced quality resident within us and call it forth into becoming–not to manipulate us but to liberate us. When another can see into our naked soul, identify some particular beauty therein, we are offered the connection we've sought so furtively. We are offered the gift of belonging.

And remember, it is a spiritual law of the universe that you cannot give what you do not have.

How to Give a Blessing

Evangelical authors Gary Smalley and John Trent have identified five elements in their study of biblical blessings: meaningful touch, spoken words, expression of high value for the one being blessed, picturing a special future for the blessee, and an active commitment on the part of the blesser to see that future realized (Smalley and Trent 1998).

---

1 For a wonderful discussion on Thomas Merton's insights about the false self and authentic self see James Finley's (1978) *Merton's Palace of Nowhere: A Search for God through Awareness of the True Self*. Notre Dame, IN: Ave Maria Press.

Building on these insights and my own years of practice, here are some suggestions on how we and those we serve might bless the important people in our lives.

First of all, let me remind you of our working definition of what a blessing is for our soul legacy purposes: a *blessing* is simply calling attention to a particularly special characteristic or quality in someone you love and encouraging that trait into greater realization. Telling someone you love them is good, but telling them *why* you love them is even more powerful. There is additional gravitas when a senior adult blesses because they have the perspective that only years and a life of experiences can provide. An aged person's words can have a lasting impact on younger lives for years to come.

And giving a blessing has numerous benefits for both the giver and receiver. For the giver, preparing for and offering a blessing can offer therapeutic relief from the diminishing abilities and loss of autonomy due to the aging process. Thinking about the ones you love and why you love them takes the focus away from you and your own problems. Additionally, this blessing process is a wonderful means for strengthening the relationships and roles of the senior adult–vital elements for a healing experience.

For the receiver of the blessing there are two potentially significant outcomes. First it can help provide relief as a treasured memory in the grieving process after the aged blesser dies. And second, the blessing may help shape the blessee's life for years to come.

So now we come to the question, how do I actually give a blessing? To begin, think about someone you love. Why do you love them? What is special about them? Then think of a way to tell them how special they are. You may want to write out what you want to say or simply have an idea of what you want to speak from your heart. You can offer a prayer, and share a favorite quote, song, or poem.

It is also helpful to give them a small gift or token as a memorial of your telling them why you love them so much. Your gift can be a picture, a memento, a piece of jewelry, or even something you have made. If you're a woodworker, knitter, or scrapbooker you could make something specially designed for this occasion. Even a collection of family recipes is wonderful.

I'm not that good with crafts myself. But on one of my son's important birthdays I gathered some of my favorite quotes–words and thoughts by famous people I find particularly important for living a good life. I also went to his Facebook page and downloaded some of the pictures he had posted. I put the quotes and pictures into a little booklet for him I made at a local copy store. Of all the gifts I've given him over the years, that one elicited a deep and memorable bonding moment for both of us. What I'm trying to say is that any creative way you can communicate your love is wonderful.

So, once you have an idea of what you want to say and have chosen a token to mark the event, you can think about the where and when to give your gifts. Threshold times in the life of your loved one–weddings, graduations, holidays, important birthdays or anniversaries–are wonderful opportunities to give a blessing. You may choose to give your blessing publicly or privately, but consider not wanting to embarrass the one you are blessing.

However you choose to impart your blessing should be congruent with your relationship to the blessee. You can ritualize the event by lighting a candle, burning some incense, or having special music playing in the background. Sharing some favorite food you both enjoy is another idea. The more personal you can make the moment, the better. Let your love and creativity guide you.

When you actually give the blessing, you might physically touch them (in an appropriate way) as you give your blessing. Holding hands, or placing your hands on their shoulder or head (if that is comfortable for the blessee), can add richness to the moment. And this is very important– look at them. Deeply look at them in the eyes. See them. Communicate your love and appreciation of them with your very soul. The *way* you communicate what you have planned to share is just as important as *what* you share. And don't rush the moment. Savor it. This is a celebration of love.

Giving a blessing doesn't have to be as elaborate as I've just suggested. These are just best-case scenarios to share with the senior adults you work with. The hospice patients I work with certainly don't have the time and energy for such well-planned-out and crafted behests. But that doesn't mean they can't still give their blessings to loved ones; it just becomes a much simpler process.

For example, I remember meeting Jim and his family. Jim had worked hard all of his life, loved hunting and fishing, and was never big on organized religion. So his family was somewhat surprised when he agreed to see the hospice chaplain. He was a tall man and a plain speaker. On my first visit he told me he wasn't afraid of death, it was the dying that was wearing on his nerves. Now confined to bed with nothing to do after always being active was just hard on him. I suggested he consider giving his blessing to his family. We talked about what a blessing is as I've shared with you.

I told him, "Look, you can lie here just staring at the ceiling waiting to die, or you can think about your wife, your son, your daughter-in-law, and your grandkids–what it is that you really love about each of them and how you can tell them that–it's up to you." He took me up on my offer.

At Jim's funeral service I heard his son Dave share that Jim had not only been a great father but Dave's best friend as well, helping Dave build his home after Jim had retired. I listened as the grandsons told how Jim had taught them at an early age to hunt and fish, how important deer season with grandpa was in their growing-up years. But they also shared about their last conversations with Jim and how special he made them feel as he told them why he loved each of them so much.

A few weeks after the service I received a thank you note from Jim's daughter-in-law Ellen. It said in part:

> I'm so glad dad took your advice, and shared not only with me, but with all of his grandchildren, what he loved about them. I can't tell you how much this meant to each of our family members as well as myself. Their grandpa (and my dad) was such an important person to all of us, and him taking the time to tell each of us why we were special to him is a memory we will all cherish for the rest of our lives.

In over 40 years of ministry I have seen firsthand, as both a participant and an observer, the potent agency for transformation contained within a blessing. To give a blessing is literally an opportunity for your soul to touch the future.

No matter where those we are ministering to are on their life journey, an important part of our task as spiritual leaders is to help them prepare for a good death. Each of our parishioners and patients is going to die at some point. And trust me, dying well is much better than not. No less an authority than Henri Nouwen has written:

> If I die with much anger and bitterness, I will leave my family and friends behind in confusion, guilt, shame, or weakness. When I felt my death approaching, I suddenly realized how much I could influence the hearts of those whom I would leave behind. If I could truly say that I was grateful for what I had lived, eager to forgive and be forgiven, full of hope that those who loved me would continue their lives in joy and peace, and confident that the God who calls me would guide all who somehow belonged to my life–if I could do that–I would, in the hour of my death, reveal more true spiritual freedom than I had been able to reveal all the years of my life. I realized on a very deep level that dying is the most important act of living. It involves a choice to bind others with guilt or set them free with gratitude. (1997, p.106)

Because dying is such an important part of our living, taking a deeper look into the experience of death will be the focus of the next chapter.

9

Connecting with Mortality

Rudy was a devout atheist who regularly attended the First Presbyterian Church. Actually, that's where we met, sort of. It's not that Rudy was looking to convert from atheism–he just loved to sing, and being in the Presbyterian choir gave him a chance to share the beauty of his deep bass voice.

The pastor was out of town one Sunday and had asked me to preach for her. The next day Rudy knocked on my office door at the hospital. After a brief introduction I thought he had come because he had been captivated by the brilliance of my sermon. I soon discovered he was on a mission and this interview was a test.

During the sermon I had mentioned I was a hospice chaplain. Rudy had come to check out my views on advance directives and set me straight if I didn't see things as he did. His wife had died after years of dementia, and the toll it had taken on him and his children (both emotionally and financially) caring for her body long after her mind, memories, and anima had vacated was devastating. After retiring from a distinguished career of psychiatry, Rudy now spent his days working to help people plan for their death. He had experienced firsthand the importance of making your preferences known about the kind of medical care you would and would not want to have done if you could no longer communicate for yourself. I passed Rudy's test.

He became a dear friend and mentor. Rudy was one of those rare individuals who seemed to have shed his ego and passionately enjoyed his living. Well into his 90s, he continued to learn, to read, to sing, to travel, and to enjoy the pleasures of intimacy with his beloved partner. Rudy was simply alive while always having his dying in view.

The week before he died he called me to his home and asked if I would give the eulogy at his memorial service. After pointing out the incongruity of praising an atheist in a Presbyterian church–I humbly agreed. He chuckled and handed me a folder containing what he wanted me to say. The folder contained the distilled data of his richly lived life: his résumé, his accolades, and his distinguished achievements. All facts. But what was missing from the folder was the delight he exuded when learning new discoveries about how the brain works, the passion in his eyes as he shared his thoughts about living and dying, the joy on his face while singing in a choir. What was missing from the folder was the way he made you feel special when you were with him.

Early on in our relationship Rudy sent me a letter in which he quoted Johannes Brahms from one of the pieces he loved to sing, "The German Requiem." Words Rudy's life made very real.

> "Lord, make me to know the measure of my days on earth,
> to consider my frailty that I must perish."

The Difficulty in Defining Death

In this chapter I'll share with you some of what I've learned about death and dying after more than a decade of hospice work. We'll look at some problems death poses for professional ministers, and some aids in addressing these opportunities. But before we do, I must give you a caveat: I have more questions than I do answers. Romanian-born theater of the absurd playwright Eugene Ionesco once wrote, "It is not the answer that enlightens, but the question."[1] My hope is that the questions explored in what follows will open up for you greater pathways of wisdom and compassion to aid in your ministry to the dying.

---

1   As quoted by Stuart Wells in *Choosing the Future: The Power of Strategic Thinking* (Oxford: Butterworth-Heinemann, 1998, p.15) from Ionesco's play *Découvertes* (1970).

First of all, I'd like to give you a little context. Nearly all of the folks I meet and serve are north of 70 years of age. Most often, people in their 80s, 90s, and even 100s. Also, I work in a relatively safe middle-class environment. By and large, the people I serve have at least had a shot at a good life. These facts very much color my experience. I'm sure chaplains who work with dying children, or in places of great poverty and privation, would have different perspectives. But, since the vast majority of contemporary North American churchgoers are made up of the population I serve, I think that what follows will be helpful in your ministry.

To begin, nearly all of the folks I work with are more afraid of dying than they are of death. The emotional struggles with their diminished autonomy, loss of meaning, the fear of pain, and the great anxiety of being a burden to loved ones far outweigh any concerns about what happens after death. The one great exception to this, in my experience, is among evangelicals who are often terrified of going to hell. But more of that in a bit.

In many ways, excluding natural disasters and armed conflict, for many in the privileged First World it has never been harder to die. This is not necessarily a good thing. It was just a mere 70 years ago or so that dying was a much simpler process. But with the advent of cardio-pulmonary resuscitation (CPR), ventilators, dialysis machines, organ transplantation, and a proliferation of antibiotics–as well as a host of surgical and genetic procedures–dying has become very complicated. One of the founders of the Zen Hospice Project in San Francisco, Frank Ostaseski, has observed:

> Medical technology has dramatically altered the dying experience. The idea of a "natural death" is slowly vanishing from our culture, having been replaced by a more antiseptic, institutionalized death managed by medical professionals... the line between who is alive and who is dead has become increasingly hazy. (2017, p.272)

We are the first generation of human beings that has ever had to wrestle with the ethical, philosophical, theological, physical, and emotional issues that are constituent with this complex dying experience.

Often pastors and chaplains can feel overwhelmed in providing guidance for patients and families through such a maze of competing issues and information. They are not alone. It is not uncommon for the various doctors and nurses involved in a patient's care to disagree on the best course of treatment. While everyone involved longs for certitude in decision making, all too often none is to be found.

One important consequence of the current complexity in end-of-life medical treatment is that, as Ostaseski states, "the line between who is alive and who is dead has become increasingly hazy." Take, for example, the case of Jahi McMath. Jahi was 13 years old when in December of 2013 she went into a hospital in Oakland, CA, for a tonsillectomy and adenoidectomy. After surgery she suffered a massive hemorrhage which led to a heart attack. Three days later she was declared brain dead. Jahi's family refused the withdrawal of life support. Even though the Alameda County coroner issued a death certificate on January 3, 2014, Jahi's family took her to a hospital in New Jersey for further testing. Since late 2014, Jahi has been in an apartment in New Jersey where she receives support from a home ventilator. Her body has not disintegrated as many professionals had predicted. In fact, her young teenage body continues to develop. And in at least 22 video-recorded instances, Jahi has moved appropriate body parts to verbal cues (Muramoto 2017).

In California Jahi is legally dead. In New Jersey she is alive. What do you say? How would you counsel her family?

As bioethicists, philosophers, and medical experts contend with complex cases like Jahi's, two central issues are emerging. The first is developing an understanding of what constitutes a person (Lizza 2006). Is a person distinct from and more than merely a biological organism (a body)? This leads to a second field of inquiry under consideration which is developing multiple criteria for what constitutes death (Lizza 2006; Berkson 2016).

All of this may read like science fiction to you, but this is the state of our current healthcare reality. And it is rapidly and constantly changing.

So how can we as professional ministers provide spiritual guidance for patients and families going through such a web of confusion? First of all, we can refrain from trying to provide definitive answers with the certitude of conviction for complexities beyond our knowing. This is not to say we are to simply stand by in silence as observers of the unfolding drama. I trust that whatever faith tradition in which you are rooted offers wisdom and guidance for difficult times. But what the dying have taught me is they really don't want rote answers or unexperienced information. What they desire is someone to be with them who may not have definitive solutions but is comfortable in being with them in the terrifying unknown and letting them work it out for themselves. They want someone who has struggled with these issues for her or himself, who has wrestled with their own existential demons, and now walks with a limp (see Genesis 32). By not imposing our personal doctrinal beliefs on a dying person but rather by inviting them into the present moment of disorienting reality and companioning with them in this scary place with our own fears in tow, true compassion is possible. Pema Chödrön teaches:

> Compassion is not a relationship between the healer and the wounded. It's a relationship between equals. Only when we know our own darkness well can we be present for the darkness of others. Compassion becomes real when we recognize our shared humanity. (Chödrön and Seu 2002, p.73)

I have learned that being present in such a profound way with a dying person actually helps me become more human.

Belden Lane, a St. Louis University theology professor, was caring for his dying mother in a nursing home when he learned:

> All theologizing, if worth its salt, must submit to the test of hospital gowns, droning television sets, and food spilled in the clumsy effort to eat. What can be said of God that may be spoken without shame in the presence of those who are dying? (2007, p.35)

Selah.

Sinners in the Hands of an Angry God

Giving an explanation for death and offering ways to prepare well for it are major themes of all the world's great religions (Bianchi 1992). But what happens when those explanations terrify folks with the belief they will burn for all eternity in hell? In my experience, this fear is a terror most frequently voiced by evangelical Christians. Of the nearly 2000 dying patients I have served, if I were to list the 50 persons who had the most difficult time dying–exhibited by real fear of the afterlife (hell) and mean-spirited demands of family and friends–more than half of them self-described as evangelical or fundamentalist Christians. And evangelicals comprise less than 20 percent of the folks I meet professionally. Now I realize this is purely anecdotal evidence and not rigorous research. Still, nearly 2000 is a good sample size.

So, the question that begs asking is, "Why?"

My own thinking revolves around three core components: a judgment-based theology, a harsh God concept (see Chapter 6), and an inability to forgive oneself (see Chapter 7). I suggest it is some combination of these three factors that causes such dread for individuals as death draws near. The one common symptom among such persons is a very strong unfulfilled desire to earn God's acceptance. The inability to simply receive God's grace and the never-ending efforts to earn it leads to no shortage of spiritual suffering.

While such situations are often difficult, they also provide an opportunity for real ministry. I have learned that challenging someone's deeply held theological understanding, even if it is causing torment, is not productive. Research suggests that people often gravitate to a theological position and God concept based upon how they feel about themselves (Benson and Spilka 1973). Therefore, my approach in ministering to one suffering from the fears of hell is to begin by offering acceptance of who they are. As an agent of religion, my hope is that if the person I am serving can sense my loving acceptance, they will then be able to consider the possibility that God (however harsh their concept) loves and accepts them as well. Once trust is built, we may then be able to explore any possible needs for forgiveness. It is from this place of forgiveness and loving acceptance that theological alternatives can be offered.

It is important here to restate that the goal is not to impose our beliefs on the person we are called to serve. It is to help them find their own way through their dying process and relationship with God. Ostaseski puts it so well, that "when people are dying, they need intensive care–intensive love, intensive compassion, and intensive presence. Ultimately, spiritual support is the fearless commitment to honor the individual's unique way of meeting death" (2017, p.268). While we cannot make individuals who fear God's wrath receive God's love, we can certainly proclaim the Sacred One's loving acceptance. Of course, this demands that we have received it ourselves. Remember, as I have shared several times, we cannot give what we do not have. Dying people have a keen sense about what is authentic. If we try to present a loving acceptance or peace about the dying process that we do not internally connect with, they will know it.

The Dying Well Paradox

So here is the great paradox for preparing to die well: contemplating death helps us live fully engaged lives now–and living fully engaged lives now is the best preparation for death. As I've shared earlier, contemplating death–being mindful of our finitude–can awaken us to appreciate the moments we now have and intentionally live our lives to the fullest. Death awareness can be a powerful antidote to the nonsense which assaults our lives on a daily basis. It can liberate us to accurately discern what is important and that which is not. Such intentional living is a great aid in mitigating regrets as death actually approaches. As Thoreau so famously stated, "I do not want to die without having lived" (Manning 2000, p.145). Helping those we serve to become fully alive is one of the most important functions of religious ministry. Again, this requires us to become alive ourselves.

Poet Christian Wiman puts it succinctly (as poets tend to do), writing that "Death is here to teach us something, or to make us fit for something" (2013, p.105). And Erich Lindemann adds:

> If you can begin to see death as an invisible, but friendly, companion on your life's journey, gently reminding you to not wait until tomorrow to do what you mean to do–then you can learn to *live* your life rather than simply passing through it. (Hudson 1999, p.95)

Seeing death as a benevolent teacher flies in the face of our cultural death myths. Yet something deep within us knows this to be true. Henri Nouwen gives voice to this inner resonance: "I have a deep sense, hard to articulate, that if we could really befriend death, we would be free people" (Nouwen and Durback 1989, p.190). The contemplation of death can set us free to live authentic lives.

End-of-Life Spiritual Care: FAQs

Over the years pastor friends have asked me numerous questions to enhance their own ministry to terminal congregants and their families. The intent of these paragraphs is not to provide boiler plate responses for difficult end-of-life situations. Rather, my hope is that what I present, as honestly as I can, will inspire your own creativity for your particular ministry setting and help you better serve those in your spiritual care.

How do you relate to a dying person who has no faith in the context of a family who do? Jim was extremely resistant to faith of any sort for his whole life, but his wife Mary was a firm believer. She wanted me to visit, but when I did Jim wanted to end the conversation quickly. Mary wanted a pastor there, basically at every up and down of Jim's dying process, but the dying man didn't. I really thought of it as visiting her...but she really wanted him to be the focus.

This situation, which does frequently occur and is a classic case of spiritual triangulation, highlights one of the major distinctions I made in the Introduction addressing the difference between a pastor and a chaplain. It would violate the chaplain code of ethics if I were to proselytize Jim, or try to convert him. Yet, as a pastor there is an expectation by your ordaining faith community and parishioners that you offer your tradition or denomination's responses to Mary's desires. Additionally, in the emotionally charged atmosphere of a loved one's dying, trying to confront deeply held doctrinal beliefs is nearly always futile if not hurtful.

So what do I do? I try to be as honest with each person as I can while honoring their beliefs. When I'm with Jim I tell him that Mary wants me to talk with him about getting right with God, or saved, or making peace with his Maker (whatever language they use in their relationship) and to say that's what Mary wants. I try to do this in a way that does not put Jim on the spot or belittle Mary's desire. I want to honor what is important to Jim. I let Jim tell me what he wants and follow that lead. I want Jim to know I support him and accept him just as he is.

When I'm with Mary I'll work to help her consider the more grace-filled elements of her doctrinal background and pray with her for Jim's relationship with God. I usually pray something like: "God, however it is that you and Jim have communicated over the years of his life, however you two talk, in the deepest place of who he is I ask that you let him know how much you love him and that God you make yourself known to him."

My goal is to help all concerned navigate through this emotionally charged time without hurting each other, trusting that in the days to come there will be time, space, and clarity of thought to reframe these moments in a grace-filled light.

I never know whether to awaken someone who is sleeping, especially if they are heading downhill...and whether or how to touch them appropriately.

Neither do I. What I do in such situations depends on a number of factors, including: my previous, if any, relationship with the person, what I know about how well they did or slept the previous night, and how I'm personally feeling. If I know them well enough to know they enjoy my company I will try to wake them up, as long as someone hasn't told me they had a bad night the previous night. If that's not the case I might cough lightly or say their name softly or gently touch their hand to let them know someone is in the room with them.

I never touch someone without first asking their permission. And then it is most often just holding hands. I offer mine first, palm up, to give them the power position.

As an off-the-chart introvert my natural inclination is to not invade someone's space. So, if I have never met them before, I usually just sit for about 20 minutes and pray for them. If I know their faith tradition I pray appropriate prayers in line with that belief system; if not, I simply pray prayers of blessing.

This question really touches on the existential issue of uncertainty I talked about in Chapter 1. Almost always, after such visits I second guess myself all the way back to my car. Should I have woken them up? Should I have coughed louder? What else could I have done for them? I second guess myself a lot and have come to realize over the years it is just part of the ministry–battling those voices in my head that I'm not good enough.

What do you do with someone who doesn't want to talk about death and dying?

I don't push them into it. I have found it is much better to simply invite people into conversation, and if they don't want to play I don't push it. I don't like it when people try to push stuff onto me.

If a person, even in the final few days of life, wants me to pray for their healing, I do. Why not? I want them to know I am on their side and support them. I also trust that disease and death will eventually break through their defenses and denial and most likely at some point they will want to talk about dying. I've learned from my friend Death, you can run but you can't hide. My hope is that if I have faithfully supported them all along they may even want to talk with me about it.

In my experience it is often the family members of the dying person who don't want to talk about death. The dying person usually does. Either way, I don't push it.

The thing that pops into my mind about this is something I'm sure you see with regard to hospice care. People wait until the last minute, very often, before reaching out for pastoral care. (Just like they wait to connect with hospice care.) This mostly occurs with people who are not solidly in the community. People we know, we know. But people sometimes have the idea that a family member needs a visit from a minister, and by the time they call, and I go see what is up, the person is beyond even having a conversation. Sometimes beyond knowing someone is visiting them. Prayers are said, and not that that means nothing, but had contact been made earlier in the dying process, more could have happened.

This is frustrating, but I've learned that trying to push or talk folks into something before they are ready is usually fruitless if not hurtful. One note about praying for folks who are "beyond conversation" or are uncommunicative is that they most likely can hear everything we say. On my first day of chaplain training many years ago I was taught that the sense of hearing is the last thing we lose in the dying process. So, I always speak as if the person I am visiting can understand me. I introduce myself, explain who I am and why I am visiting, and ask permission to pray. I feel that is only polite. I also look for facial or other physical clues to see if permission is granted.

Another thing I've learned over the years is that when I ask for permission to pray with someone, if they are able to respond, how I phrase the question is very important. Now remember, most of the people I visit don't know me. We do not have a longstanding relationship. So, they can be a little wary of my request, fearful I might try to convert them or make them feel guilty. If I ask "Can I pray for you?" they often get a fearful look in their eye like "OK, here it comes, he's been nice but now he's going to get me!" So in recent years I have asked, "Can I say a prayer *of blessing* for you?" No one has ever turned me down. It seems nearly everyone is more open to receiving a blessing than some kind of unknown prayer.

As you point out though, the earlier we can be invited to provide ministry the more we have to offer. Research shows that people who go onto hospice care early actually live longer than those who pursue aggressive treatment and have a much better quality of life (Pyenson *et al.* 2004; Connor *et al.* 2007). Additionally, early hospice care reduces the depression experienced by grieving survivors after the loved one's death (Ornstein *et al.* 2015).

I think the places that I get "tripped up" have to do with family dynamics and often having to work with family members who I do not know and relationships that are fractured in ways that I do not know and being sure I honor the person who is dying in the midst of all of that...

The family systems theorists teach that this is very common to occur at the time of a family member's death. I simply try to do spiritual triage, working to make sure as little emotional damage is done as possible to all of the actors, and hoping that when the dust settles there will be time to more intentionally work on whatever issues are in play. It's just too hard to sort through many longstanding family secrets and dynamics in the middle of a storm. But the storm can crack open the façade and let light in for future ministry.

And then there's the practical thing–sometimes someone is gravely ill for months and I have lots of work to do for a lot of people–so, being sure I stay in touch without being over-extended...

This is where having pastoral care teams is so helpful. We do not have to be the only ones providing spiritual support. Where I work, I am the only full-time chaplain. Sometimes, patients either don't like me or are uncomfortable with an older white man visiting them. But I still want to help ensure they are spiritually well cared for. In my situation, working with the social workers, nurses, and aides means I can stay in touch with the patient's situation and offer suggestions to my colleagues on how they can help address any spiritual issues that arise.

As a pastor, you can do the same with associates or lay pastoral care teams. Instead of working directly with the dying person or their family, you pastor the care givers. As Jethro wisely told his son-in-law Moses, get some help in caring for these folks or you're going to drive yourself crazy (Exodus 18.17ff, NIV).

Having just watched my mother die, you could say this: death, even that of a saint, may not look like what you think it will. It can be traumatizing... What do we suppose the dying person is experiencing? Where/how does God fit into the experience of death? Are loved ones supposed to feel a certain way?

Yes, death, particularly that of a loved one, can be traumatizing. When you are emotionally involved, whether it is a family member or a dear friend, trying to provide spiritual care may not be wise. You are in need of support yourself and should be afforded the space to grieve.

As to what a dying person is experiencing–that is a great mystery. Many of the folks I have cared for see long-deceased loved ones. These used to be called hallucinations, but no longer are called so. Many studies have been done from around the world where people of numerous cultures, economic classes, and ethnicities have had the same experiences–long-deceased loved ones appear who do not frighten the dying person–experiences that defy an accurate classification of what the experience actually is.

I remember one man I served who had this experience and it did shake him. He had been a devout atheist, a philosopher from Harvard who was certain that when we die we simply cease to exist. He was very old and tired and in pain and just longed for that non-existence. Several weeks before he died his mother and father appeared to him. It caused him to reevaluate his entire life philosophy: what if there is an afterlife after all? But he was the exception. Most dying people I have worked with find these experiences comforting.

Where is God in the experience of dying? I believe, right in the thick of it. The biblical verse I pray with nearly every patient I serve is from Hebrews 13.5: "For God has said, never will I leave you, never will I forsake you" (NIV). Granted, that is my belief. But it is a conviction that empowers me to do this kind of work. I could not represent a God who abandons us when we need her or him most.

As to what families feel as they watch a loved one die, usually it is a mixture of sadness, grief, and a desire for it to hurry up and be over with. That last feeling is the cause for a lot of unfounded guilt–which I always try to defuse. Watching someone you love suffer or labor at dying is unnerving. Wanting it to end quickly is a very natural and humane reaction.

Many families also struggle with feelings of inadequacy, that they are not doing enough. One of the most important aspects of my ministry is to encourage family members in the care they are providing. To help them focus on what they are doing as opposed to what they are not. I often say something like: "Right now there are more than seven billion people on planet Earth. I don't know how many of those seven billion will die this week (or month), but of all those who will die, how many can say they are safe, warm, not in pain, and surrounded by people who love them? There are people who will die in refugee camps, on the streets of places like Manila or Calcutta, in ICUs with tubes jammed in their bodily orifices, or alone and forgotten. Your loved one is not dying that way because of what you are providing. You are giving them everything that is really important at this time of life." This usually helps family members relax and appreciate what they are doing for the one they love.

When you first meet or talk with someone who is dying, what do you say?

I think the most significant thing I try to do when I meet someone who is dying is to treat them like a normal person. I work to insulate myself from all of the information the hospice team or family tries to give me about the patient's disease. I don't want that information (unless it is contagious). I'm not meeting prostate cancer or Alzheimer's or COPD (chronic obstructive pulmonary disease)–I'm meeting Bill or Mary, someone who loves, someone who has hopes and dreams and fears.

So, I often begin the conversation talking about things we might share in common. What is your favorite sports team? What kind of books do you like to read? Movies? What are your favorite foods? (See Ostaseski 2017.) My intention is to lead with our shared humanity. I'm intentionally trying to communicate that I'm not here to fix them or change them but rather to companion with them on their unique journey.

Now, as the conversation progresses, there are several questions I have come to rely on to help me assess how I might serve this person. For example, "What's your understanding of what's happening to you?" (Jenkinson 2015). This clues me in on how my patient views their situation and how it matches the reality of what is actually going on. I don't try to challenge what they say or try to change it. I simply honor it and use what they tell me as a place to begin our relationship.

Another helpful question is: "As you think about the next several weeks, does anything worry you?" Or conversely: "As you think about the next several weeks, is there anything you hope for?" After asking one or both of these questions, I stay silent for several minutes and let my patient respond if and how they want to. I don't say anything and just wait. These questions simply help me assess what is really important to the dying person, so that I can support their wishes. I often have to fight the temptation that I really know what they need. But it's their life, and death, not mine. I don't want to be manipulative but rather want to support and honor their struggle.

One of the biggest issues I've seen that causes tension with families as someone is dying involves trying to feed the dying person when they don't want to eat.

Yes, this is often a cause for family strife as a loved one is dying. As death nears, the desire and need for food and fluids diminishes. Usually the dying person is bedridden and is thus burning very few calories, so the need for food is much less than for an active healthy person. And at some point with the shutting down of bodily functions, even the ability to digest food will cease. Therefore, forcing food into someone in this condition can cause discomfort if not harm.

Often the tension is between family members who live afar and local family members. The long-distance family members cannot physically see how much their loved one has deteriorated and have images of the dying person (looking robust in their memory) being starved to death. In such cases I try to educate the family on what is happening physically with the dying loved one and will even give out literature explaining the situation (Zitter 2014).

To be honest, sometimes it helps and sometimes not.

What can you tell me about the forms that are used to communicate end-of-life wishes?

There are two primary forms used in the United States that people utilize to communicate end-of-life wishes in case they at some point become incapacitated. The first is simply called an Advance Directive, and these vary slightly from state to state. The basic idea is that you write down your preferences for things like CPR (cardio-pulmonary resuscitation), feeding tubes, and other significant interventions to lengthen your life at all costs. A key element of an Advance Directive is that you name a medical power of attorney to speak on your behalf if you become unable to speak for yourself. You choose, normally a family member you trust, to be your advocate if necessary.

The other form is called a POLST (Physician's Orders for Life-Sustaining Treatment), which covers the same basic questions as an Advance Directive. The big difference is that only your doctor can fill out a POLST.

The real problem is that both of these forms are often set aside or disregarded if one of your family members shows up at the hospital and threatens to sue if everything is not done at all costs to lengthen your life. For example, where I live, in southern Oregon, one doctor has told me that advance directives are followed by the medical team only about 25 percent of the time. So the most important thing you can do to communicate what you do and do not want to happen at the end of your life if you are unable to speak for yourself is tell your family members *now*. The forms are important, but communicating with your loved ones is more important.

I'm a DNR–as in "Do Not Resuscitate."

To be honest, the reasons why I don't want CPR are a mixture of both faith and fear. Faith that whatever happens after this life is really good, and fear that those who pound on my chest may be able to restart my heart but may not be able to bring my brain back with it.

Contrary to what you may have seen in the movies and on TV, most of the time, CPR doesn't end well. In fact, more than 95 percent of the time (Murray 2012). And it's worse than on those rare occasions when in the movies someone simply dies–much worse.

If you're young, healthy, and if the CPR is performed within minutes of your heart stopping, your chances of recovery for a meaningful life are good. But there are a lot of "ifs" in that last sentence. And if, on the other hand, you're older and more than a few minutes go by without oxygen getting to your brain, your chances of ever leaving a healthcare institution are really slim (less than 3%), and the decisions your loved ones will have to make are really horrific.

Many patients who have had CPR end up on a ventilator (a mechanical device that forces the body to breathe and move the needed oxygen to vital body parts). All too often, however, the real damage has already been done and the brain can no longer tell the body what to do. So somewhere between 8 and 14 days after an expensive and ventilated stay in an ICU, the doctors will ask your family if they want to have a "trach" and feeding tube inserted into you. You, of course, are completely sedated because your care providers don't want you to reflexively yank the very uncomfortable plastic tube out of your throat that is necessary for oxygen flow. Because of fears of infection, the tracheotomy is now needed. It's a small hole cut into your throat to insert a more permanent tube to force your body to breathe. The feeding tube is necessary to force nutrients into your system. Without these, you will die. So now your family must make the awful decision to "pull the plug" (stop treatment) or go ahead with the "trach" and feeding tube while you are left to linger in this in-between state for only God knows how long. This is the stuff they never show you on the TV shows. And this happens all too frequently in nearly every hospital in the country.

For your loved ones, these decisions are awful. They often feel a lot like the old story of the frog in the kettle. The heat keeps getting turned up slowly until the water is boiling and the frog is cooked. In this case, your family is made to feel like the frog by listening to hourly or daily reports on your progress or lack thereof and then having to decide if you live or die. But you're not really living–just lying on a bed with machinery making your body do things your brain used to tell it to do when it was working.

Under no circumstances do I want my family to have to make these kinds of decisions, so that's why I'm a DNR. I've told them I love them, my life is so much richer for having loved them, but if Jesus comes to take me to that place where the Bible says there is no more suffering, or tears, or crying, or pain (see Revelation 21.4, NIV)–then under no circumstances try and bring me back. I'll be just fine, and waiting for them.

Conclusion

In over a decade working as a hospice chaplain, I have seen the existential issues addressed in the first two chapters of this book played out again and again in the lives of dying patients. The great difficulty is that these issues are not only complex and multilayered, but all too often the people I serve in hospice care no longer have the physical stamina or mental acuity to adequately wrestle with them.

Therefore, my plan was to develop a mechanism to help senior adults begin to address these inevitable existential concerns long before the diagnosis of a serious or life-threatening illness. To this end, I have developed a seminar to aid senior adults in the process of crafting a soul legacy to have as a foundation for their eventual end-of-life process and a gift to be passed onto surviving loved ones. As I have shared, the elements in my recipe for the seminar include: connecting with your soul, your story, the Sacred, others, and your mortality.

A corollary aim of the seminar is that those participants who upon reflection of their life are dissatisfied with their soul's legacy will still be able to make changes by investing in meaningful experiences and relationships while they have the health, time, and energy to do so.

The way I presented this concept to prospective attendees was by sharing that they probably have a financial will to disperse monetary assets at their eventual time of death, but what about their soul's assets? Who will inherit those, and how? And just as a financial will can be modified every few years, so too can their soul's legacy be adjusted and modified as life and relationships warrant. This seminar is simply an opportunity to begin the process of crafting such a legacy of the soul.

What follows in the next chapter is a synopsis of the seminar as it was experienced by over 30 senior adults in the spring of 2014 at three different venues.

10

The Soul Legacy Seminar

The assignment for week two was to either tell a story from your life or write a fairy tale about your life. Jenny wrote a fairy tale.

The fairy tale was about a mother lion that had an infection and wanted to help her cubs by sharing her life story. As the infection grew the mother lion needed to rely on others for help, and this was very hard for her, as she had always been so self-sufficient.

The mother lion was very proud of her cubs, both of whom eventually fell in love with other lions and got married, having cubs of their own. The mother lion was happy for them but sad because she wouldn't be part of their lives much longer due to the infection. She relished her cubs teaching their grandmother's life lessons and story. "It was like a dream come true," she shared.

Jenny concluded by sharing, "I'm losing my memory... I have early-onset Alzheimer's, so I tell my children my stories while I can remember them. I so want them to hold onto my stories and lessons."

Jenny was one of 34 participants in a five-week pilot study which formed the basis of my doctoral dissertation incorporating many of the concepts in this book. In this chapter I'll share a synopsis of that program, significant responses from the participants, and plans for the development of a multi-week program faith communities and continuing care facilities can utilize to help senior adults prepare for dying a good death.

The original Soul Legacy Seminar program was approved by the IRB (Institutional Review Board) at the Pacific School of Religion in Berkeley, CA, and was also approved by representatives of three host sites. Participation was solicited from four social communities in the Rogue Valley of southern Oregon: a United Church of Christ (UCC), an American Baptist (AB) church, a Continuing Care Retirement Community (CCRC), and a senior adult Lifelong Learning Institute (LLI). The LLI opted not to present the program to their constituents. The remaining three sites were selected for their diversity of worldviews: the UCC church is theologically and culturally more liberal, the AB church more conservative, and the CCRC is more diverse in both of these areas. Additionally, I have a standing relationship with all three communities. Permission to conduct the program with the three sites was given and participants were recruited with the help of the UCC pastor, the AB pastor, and the chaplain director of pastoral services from the CCRC. Eligibility for the program required the participants to meet the following criteria: (1) must be at least 50 years of age, (2) must commit to attending all five sessions of the program, and (3) must have the mental acuity to participate in group discussions and commit to preparing materials for these discussions. A maximum of 13 participants was set for each class to ensure ample time for sharing. The two church pastors and director of pastoral services from the CCRC selected possible candidates for the program who were then contacted by the author and given a written description of the program with appropriate permission forms. Seven possible candidates declined to participate in the program.

A total of 34 adults participated, including one married couple. The participants ranged in age from 53 to 93, 70.5 percent were retired, and 61.7 percent were female. Eleven participants were married, ten were widowed, three were divorced, and three were single. Ten of the participants had graduated from high school, ten had graduated from college, and 14 had graduate degrees. Most of the sample said they were Christian (22), three said they were agnostic, and nine said they were eclectic (Grewe 2016, pp.5-6).

Week One: Connecting with Your Soul

Prior to the first session each participant was given the exercise in Appendix B to prepare for the class. Each person in the group then shared for about five minutes what they put in their Soul Print Box and why. Here are some of the significant responses from the exercise:

- This is a letter from our oldest son thanking his parents for how we raised him; this letter I would never, never part with...

- This is an email from a friend, my first friend. I was a lonely isolated kid and got a scholarship to an art class where I met my friend...his friendship changed my life dramatically. In college we were roommates...he is a pianist and I sing; we did recitals...

- My mother's Bible. She bought it with her last few dollars from a door-to-door salesman. It was special to her and what she taught me. I loved finding what she underlined, a flower from my wedding was in it. And this is a little dress I wore as a child, my aunt kept it and it reminds me of love, because my aunt kept it, my mother made it for me, and my aunt perserved it...

Week Two: Connecting with Your Story

At the end of the first session the exercise in Appendix C was handed out in preparation for the following week's class. Here are some of the significant responses from the exercise:

- I got fired from my job...friends helped me find work, they were tough times but I experienced great growth that forged my life themes: relationship with God and inner strength. The four lessons I want to pass on to my kids and grandkids are: 1. when faced with daunting experiences, don't give up, 2. never underestimate the value of friends and family, so nurture those relationships beyond all else, 3. maintain faith in yourself even when outside forces seem to be against you, and 4. nurture your faith in God. I'm still wrestling with what I am doing now–is it really worthwhile?

- Why I am currently the way I am, because I was a troubled person. I was desperate for positive change, dysfunctional family, absentee parents, middle of three boys, because of insecurity and lack of supervision led to "malevolent teasing among us." Think of Columbine shootings and *Lord of the Flies* by Golding. My ability to function in the world was impacted mentally, physically, emotionally, and spiritually by all of this. Therefore my life has been spent in trying to heal...one of the saving graces for me at age 21 I found solace in asking Christ into my heart, and at 32 I came closer to Christ when meeting my wife who was a Christian...

- At 17 I had cancer...that changed my life. I went through cobalt treatment for over a year. I wanted to graduate so I stopped treatment. They told me I wouldn't survive, so I told them to cut my leg off. They did. I was the only one in my family to graduate. I'm ornery... I wanted to chase the rainbow and have done that all my life. I've traveled the world. I've been a problem solver, I've made and developed prosthetics for others and had my own businesses... I'm always looking for a challenge. When I get knocked down I always get back up...

- In junior high kids were unkind, they called me "kike" and "Jew girl." I was Baptist, I was Arab-American, and I looked Jewish. Mom was Irish from the South and Dad was Syrian and Lebanese, first generation. He fled persecution. Mom told me one day you'll understand... Mom put notes in my lunch every day through college...she died from a stroke. Twice she spoke to me "I go away and I love you." She died in my arms... We promised each other we'll never be alone.

Week Three: Connecting with the Sacred

At the end of the second session the exercise in Appendix D was handed out in preparation for the following week's class. Here are some of the significant responses from that exercise:

- God is the power behind all of creation, I once spent a night on a hill...that night was a place of extreme darkness but of great power. A piece of that power came down through me and into my hands...it was a life-changing experience. I felt like I touched the face of God...it was a dazzling darkness... I realized we're all interconnected and when I am aware of that I am aware of the presence of God.

- I watched a video of the Big Bang...what caught me was the inclination of matter to group together...we are all intimately connected and when I see a bird fly, and remember that these are atoms that joined together...that's me...

- Since I am not a person of faith, the closest I can come to the Divine is miracles. I do believe in miracles. I think everything I encounter is a miracle–the presence of the Universe, the presence of life, another miracle is that we can understand some of it, how the universe began, how light works, how gravity works...

- This was a challenge for me, because when I was growing up in a Baptist family, images were verboten...20 years ago I had a sabbatical at Ghost Ranch, the landscape is striking. I saw the images and symbols in nature. I was grieving the death of my father, he had been sick a long time. I was so astounded that while I was there by myself this grief came out. I would be walking and crying, and then I remembered, "Blessed are those that mourn for they will be comforted..."

- I have had a strange progression of the images of God or the Divine given to me because they were always exclusive and that bothered me. My own experience was always inclusive. At some point, not recently, I put the two things together. It enlarged my sense of God because everyone's "My God" was exclusive and carried so much baggage. So this bowl of water is what I call "the All" or "Infinity" and this little sponge is me. (She placed the sponge in the water.) So this is me in the infinity... I am in the water and the water is in me...and other people are also sponges in the water "the All."

Week Four: Connecting with Others

At the end of the third session the exercise in Appendix E was handed out in preparation for the following week's class. Here are some of the significant responses from the exercise:

- I thought a lot about your soul sharing, shameful, painful, beautiful story with us, your beauty, you remind me of a pearl... the ragged rough grain of sand that becomes a pearl ...so I want to honor your transformation because I feel when a person can hit bottom and come up with tools and grace and beauty they can reach out and pull someone else up with humility and beauty like no one else can...

- Your fight with cancer shows your courage. My gift to you is a heart rock I got from a hike in Arizona. I knew it was yours when I drew your name because it has roots, and lines, and cracks, and real life...and it shows your strength and solidness...

- I didn't know anybody here when I showed up, but I did notice your smile. Seeing that I was a stranger you asked if you could help, you saw that I was limping a little bit, I saw your heart. Later I learned that you lost some of your leg due to cancer when you were 14...you've said numerous times, "I don't know why things haven't worked out the way I wanted but I've been doing the best I can," and I thought, isn't that all of us?

- You have shown me something of yourself in this class that I haven't seen before. I've only seen you in the gym. Our spirituality must affect our behavior, and I have seen your interactions in the gym are beautiful and important... I have written a haiku for you because you bring joy to everyone...

Week Five: Connecting with Mortality

There was no homework assignment to prepare for the final session of the seminar. During the week five class, I simply read the Nine Contemplations of Atisha (Halifax 1997; see Appendix F) as a guided meditation for the groups. Here is a sampling of the responses:

- I have a second chance; two years ago I was diagnosed with cancer, it still feels surreal, I didn't feel sick, it felt like I was in a dream. It was terrifying. I did chemo, the cancer experience has without a doubt been the greatest gift in my adult life. Amazing. I had lost sight of my dreams, I had been divorced, had to take care of a mother with dementia, difficult teenagers at home, unhappy at my job. After the diagnosis I felt so incredibly loved. I felt it would work out fine. My spirituality blossomed, in addition to chemo I did alternative therapies and changed everything I could change in my life–the way I eat, the way I think, the way I pray, the way I relate to people. I turned around. My treatment ended last summer, now it is time to start living the rest of my life. It feels like every day is a gift, and I want to consciously choose how my life is lived...my kids were supportive...

- When you talk about material things, after you die they mean nothing... Once my parents died I had to dispose of everything. I feel like I've been preparing to die ever since...

After a time of debriefing about the meditation, time was given for participants to share what they gained from the five-week experience. Here are some of their observations:

- What I got out of this class is to continue really enjoying the physical things we have now, like washing my hands, the feeling of warm water on my hands, or hearing the little bird up in the tree when I'm walking. These physical things are what I will miss most...and being aware of them and not taking them for granted...the beautiful gifts we are given. I know I'll see my family again, in a different way, but we'll miss this earthly experience...the other thing I got out of this presentation was how much I want to more completely organize things and write letters to my children, and make arrangements to get rid of my stuff...I still have my mother's stuff...she loved it so much that I feel bad about giving it away but I'm paying every month to keep it in storage...I want to get rid of my stuff to make it easier for my children.

- I really liked getting to know and experience everyone. I really liked getting in touch with the deep feelings of what I have loved in my life–it helps me let go of everything else.

- It pushed me beyond my comfort level in terms of sharing my personal experiences and the experience of others. Class 2 (story sharing) was the most difficult.

- The diversity of all attendees, respect shown for attendees with different perspectives.

- Getting to know new people and getting to know myself better.

The most surprising aspect of the project for me was how deeply the three groups bonded. By far the majority of comments and suggestions revolved around continuing to meet together. The pastor of the AB church informed me that five of the seven members from his congregation who participated in the seminar have told him they wish we were still meeting as a group. Additionally, I know of two sets of participants (paired from the blessing exercise) who still meet regularly for coffee, more than six months after the conclusion of the class. Participants had the opportunity to anonymously provide written feelings about the five-week experience. Here are some the major take-aways they shared:

- Accelerating my getting my affairs together, sharing deeply my feelings with my kids, and helping to ensure I'm the author of my life as long as possible.

- Getting to know others at this level of sharing.

- Wounding–I realized more deeply how painful my early negative experience was.

- Death is fine.

- To share with my family how I treasure them.

- Made me do a lot of thinking through the week–reminiscing and forming conclusions for further "work."

- Living each day to the fullest.

- Keep searching.

- We did become community.

- The workshop nudged me to question my seeming need for outside validation, not that this hasn't been a life-long journey with this question. It does seem that I keep on getting the opportunity to struggle with it again...until I "get it."

- Choosing to relate a short story about me made me realize how little of that life is known to my children. My husband and I did not share our early life with them. They learned he was on that Washington march only right before he died. Thank you for alerting me to this omission.

- Before we knew what had happened, we spoke to one another of our histories, deepest thoughts, and desires. Why, sometimes, people, previously unknown to each other, would leave a meeting arm in arm, conversing warmly and smiling, clearly symptoms of spontaneous detachment from the grid. Such exhibitions of freedom and good will may very well be contagious or infectious or both.

And finally, I received this note from Jenny, whose story was shared at the beginning of this chapter:

> After the losses that I have had since coming to the CC, your "Soul's Legacy" came at the perfect time. Since my husband died and I have been diagnosed with early Alzheimer's, I have focused a lot on my children and my husband's children. How can I help them? How can I support their dreams before I can no longer do so? What do I want to pass on to them? This group has really focused on these questions. I want to pass things on to my family before I die or can no longer remember their names. I felt empowered to move from a cottage to a small apartment so that I could give special items to all of my children now as opposed to later.

Conclusions

Of the 34 people who participated in the study, 14 indicated in the pre-seminar survey as feeling "sad or scared" when considering their death or finality. At the conclusion of the five weeks, that number decreased by 64 percent to five. Most of the change occurred in the UCC group, with a decrease from eight to two. Similarly, in the UCC group those who felt "peaceful or good" about the prospect of their death increased from four in the pre-seminar survey to nine folks in the post-seminar survey, an increase of 125 percent.

On the question of where people found a sense of meaning, the most interesting result was an increase of 100 percent (from four to eight) in the area of spirituality. Most of that movement came from the CCRC group, a group not affiliated with a worshiping community.

Two questions in the survey addressed how participants felt about their lives. The first spoke to how they felt about their life in general and the second on how they felt about the difficult decisions that they had made. The results show an increase in "gratitude" of 50 percent (from eight to 12) and a decrease in the number who felt "sad" about their lives from eight to five. Surprisingly, the number of participants who felt "ambivalent" about the hard choices they had made in their lives increased from four to nine, with most of that increase occurring in the CCRC group.

And finally, those who before the seminar stated they found it "hard" to share their feelings with loved ones decreased by 50 percent, from ten to five, after having participated in the class (Grewe 2016, pp.11-12).

As I say, the most surprising aspect of this project for me was the deep bonding that took place among participants in the three groups. This was a thoroughly unanticipated outcome. My original intention was simply to aid senior adults in reflecting upon their own lives and possibly reframe significant events in order to experience more peace in their latter stages of life. The overwhelming desire by a majority of participants in each of the groups to continue meeting was unexpected.

In reflecting on this unanticipated outcome from the project, several possibilities suggest themselves. First, the groups naturally achieved what Carl Rogers has identified as necessary conditions for a growth-promoting atmosphere in human development: (1) there was a transparent genuineness exhibited by the participants in the groups, (2) a non-judgmental, "unconditional positive regard" gifted each participant with the feeling of being accepted, and (3) the groups afforded an empathetic understanding to the members (1995). While not intentionally built into the design of the seminar, this atmosphere, achieved by each of the groups, had a significant influence on the outcomes measured.

The second contributing factor to the group bonding that occurred may well be the power of story sharing. As referenced earlier in this book, story creation is a major project of the human experience. It appears that story sharing (in an atmosphere described above) promotes fertile soil for a deepening of relationships.

Finally, I do think my own comfort, as the facilitator, in considering death, dying, and the existential issues associated with them afforded the groups a degree of safety for their own exploration. This belief has been one of the main premises of this book. My hope is that what you have found within these pages has brought further peace for you as you are faced with ministering to these issues with those you serve.

As I continue to offer this seminar to other groups I am planning on adding two additional modules: one as an introduction to the existential issues as outlined in Chapter 1, and another based on the forgiveness themes in Chapter 7.

Epilogue

So, What Have I Learned?

Several years ago, after my first book was published, I was visiting with Marie at her nursing home. A beautiful woman in the early stages of dementia, Marie was a devoted Christian and ever the quintessential lady with an incredible gift of hospitality. Like a number of folks I have visited over the years with dementia, Marie, who could not remember much if any of her own story, retained her hard-wired social graces enough to ask questions about my life. It was a deflecting mechanism for keeping polite conversation going.

"So, what's new in your life?" she dutifully asked.

"Well, I've had a book published."

"Wonderful! What's it about?"

"Oh, it's just stories of memorable visits I've had with hospice patients over the years. It's called *What the Dying Have Taught Me about Living*."

"So, what have they taught you?" she asked demurely.

I was stumped. No one had ever bothered to ask me that before and I had no rehearsed little talk stream developed to explain the book. After several awkward moments I stammered out, "I guess it's to cultivate gratitude, surrender to reality, and shower the people you love with love." (Yes, I know I stole that last one from James Taylor.)

Over the years as I've reflected on my response to Marie in the nursing home and after all the years of research that have gone into crafting this book, I still stand by what tumbled out of my mouth that day. Well, nearly. I'd add one more item: live generously. I call them my spiritual vital signs.

Vital Signs

One of the drawbacks in being a minister is that nearly everyone lies to you at a first meeting. For example, when I meet a new hospice patient or their family as a chaplain and ask "How is everyone doing?" they usually all say "Fine" or "Praise God, I'm good...I'm just waiting to go to heaven."

Often those are simply deflections.

Those are the responses we're all trained to tell the minister to keep him or her far away from doing any harm. If we actually tell the truth, the minister would likely try to probe deeper and unearth all the little tawdry dark family secrets that have caused enormous pain for years–and no one wants that!

To circumvent the social niceties that deflect against getting to really know folks, I've developed a list of *spiritual vital signs* I look for to help determine what's really going on inside someone's soul. Here's my list of *spiritual vitals signs*: cultivate gratitude, live generously, surrender to reality, and shower the people you love with love. These are the qualities I look for in meeting a new patient to help me determine the health of his or her soul.

Benedictine monk David Steindl-Rast has famously promoted the mantra "Happiness does not make us grateful, but gratefulness makes us happy." A brief scan of the TED Talks library[1] gives you an indication of the growing awareness of the importance gratitude holds for spiritual and mental well-being. I've learned that gratitude is something we cultivate. It's also magnetic. The more I express gratitude, the more I find to be grateful for. Sadly, I've also learned the same is true for ingratitude. The more I bitch, the more I find to bitch about.

In recent years there has been a growing body of research to demonstrate that simply doing three kind things a day for others can help lift depression, improve sleep, and increase spiritual resilience. Generous behavior is evidence of a soul that has been humbled by the reception of grace and understands the deep connection we all have with each other. I have never met a truly generous person who was not aware of how much they have been given is a gift, and the natural response is to share that gift with others (see the story of the four lepers

1   www.ted.com/talks

in 2 Kings Chapter 7). Conversely, stinginess and a sense of entitlement are symptoms of a grace-starved soul.

By submission to reality I mean one's ability to simply and humbly accept the impermanent nature of life. All living things die. Over the years the folks I've met and served who can accept this fact generally die a much less painful death. Those who insist on fighting the inevitable, who refuse to give up when the end is in sight, often need far more analgesics (heavy-duty pain killers).

In serving nearly 2000 departed souls I have never once had someone say to me, "I wish I had gone to more football games" or "I wish I had spent more time online" or "I wish I could have gone shopping more often." What matters most to those at the end of their line are the people they love and those who love them. Jesus taught that there is no more important investment we can make in this life than loving God and those whom God places in our lives (see Mark 12.28-31). For so many years as a practicing Christian I thought this is what I needed to do to make God happy. To my joyful surprise, I have discovered that this is what truly makes me happy.

So these are my spiritual vital signs. Signs to give me an indication of how really alive someone's soul is. Are they truly awake to the wonder of life? Or are they asleep, simply eking out an existence without truly engaging this miraculous gift?

Of late I have been working to strengthen my own spiritual vital signs. I look for opportunities to be generous, especially with my time (which is very hard for me). Surrendering to the things I cannot change, battling the ones I can, and praying to know the difference between the two. As I sit for prayer in the evenings I try to reflect on at least three good things I chose to do on that particular day to benefit someone else. It can be big or little–but I want to find at least three. And I so want my life to be a blessing for others.

Today was a spectacularly beautiful fall day here in southern Oregon. The sky was as blue as you could want, without a cloud in sight. The deciduous leaves had hit their peak colors last weekend, but were still marvelous. I went for a long walk, wanting to kill two birds with one stone as they say. I figured the walk would help me get to my daily 10,000-step goal on my infernal Fitbit and I could use the time to pray fervently for some divine inspiration. I wanted to concoct an utterly brilliant conclusion for this book. You know, something that would make you just sit back in awe of how wise and spiritual I am.

Shortly into the walk I realized this ego-driven desire was simply the voice of that frightened little boy who still resides deep in my soul. He so wants a place to fit and to feel special.

Fortunately for both of us, no whiz-bang ending arrived. As I walked home beneath the beauty of the fading fall day I came to the realization that all I seek at this point in my life is to be a good man. I want to spend my remaining days telling the people I love why I love them. I want to reflect back to them the beauty I see within them. I want to be a conduit of God's grace rather than a participant in the fear of "not enough." I want to be kind and generous–trusting that if I give myself to these tasks I might really become the man God dreams me to be. I want at the end of my days as I lie on my deathbed for the last words that cross my lips to be "Thank you."

Appendix A

Suggestions for Group Study

Here are some suggestions for creating a small group environment suitable for addressing the existential issues presented in this book. Think of it as gathering traveling companions on a soul safari. From the following suggestions, feel free to pick and choose what seems right for you and your life context. Modify, edit, delete, add, and subtract as you see fit. After all, it's your journey.

One of the first things to consider is, what type of traveling companions do you want? It's a good idea to know what kind of trip you want to take before setting off. For example, if you're heading off to the beach, you take certain types of clothes and equipment. If going mountain climbing, you take another type of gear. This guide has been prepared to work for church groups, grief groups, and life-enrichment groups. The choice is yours. But knowing what you want to achieve is important before launching out. Considering where you want to go will influence who you invite to come along.

If you're looking for a deepening of spirituality, you might start a church group. Maybe you've recently suffered a loss or have a number of friends who have–then you might start a grief group. Or maybe if you just want to explore ways of living more intentionally and passionately, then a life-enrichment group would work.

Another aid in establishing the kind of group you want to help facilitate is thinking about the objectives for the group. Here are some of the goals I had in mind when working on the book:

- Reframe experiences of suffering to aid in growth.

- Become more accepting of self and others.

- Grow in wisdom and compassion.

- Become less afraid of dying.

- Demystify the dying process.

- Offer concrete suggestions on choices for living now to avoid the pain of regret later.

- Avoid providing simplistic answers to existential dilemmas but rather invite others to embrace life's deep questions and be changed by them.

- Discuss skills to provide a non-anxious presence for dying loved ones.

- Explore perspectives from various theologians and faith traditions and different cultures on the topic of dying.

- Present reflective tools to think about your own dying.

- Explore the difference between healing and cure.

- Present specific methods to use in alleviating suffering caused by loss of meaning.

- Share specific verbal and non-verbal skills to enhance difficult end-of-life conversations.

- Discover with others ways to enrich your life by exploring topics like gratitude, surrender, compassion, forgiveness, and trust.

- Share the power the stories we tell ourselves have over our quality of living.

- Explore the opportunities grief affords for richer living.

- Consider ways to improve your soul's health.

Now don't get intimidated. This list is not a recipe for all the things you should cover in your group. It's just a list of suggestions. Choose maybe three or four that really speak to you and see who else may be interested in joining along.

Once you've decided on the type of study group you want to facilitate and you've identified three or four objectives for the group, begin to think about the environment you want to help create for your group's exploration. Now here I'm talking about more than where you'll meet and when–I'm talking about creating a safe and accepting space where folks can feel free to roam around their souls. Henri Nouwen describes this idea beautifully when he writes about hospitality:

> Hospitality is not to change people, but to offer them space where change can take place. It is not to bring men and women over to our side, but to offer freedom not disturbed by dividing lines... The paradox of hospitality is that it wants to create emptiness, not a fearful emptiness; but a friendly emptiness where strangers can enter and discover themselves as created free; free to sing their own songs, speak their own languages, dance their own dances; free also to leave and follow their own vocations. Hospitality is not a subtle invitation to adopt the life style of the host, but the gift of a chance for the guests to find their own. (1986, pp.71-72)

This type of environment doesn't just naturally happen when folks get together, and it isn't a matter of luck–it takes intentionality on the part of the facilitators or hosts. Any group will respond to the tone of leaders. In fact, the depth of sharing and open vulnerability a group explores is dependent on how deep and honest the leaders are. Something to think about.

So, to help create this kind of safe and accepting atmosphere, it's a good idea to present some agreements that everyone in the group will understand and buy into before you begin:

Here are some suggestions:

- We will be respectful.

- We will speak our truth with sensitivity to other people's truth. While our perspectives may differ, we will not interpret, correct, or debate what others share. We want to speak from our authentic selves, using "I" statements, and trusting others to hear with discernment.

- We will not trash others. This is not the forum to discuss or complain about politics, our church, our family, or our co-workers.

- We will not try to fix, to save, and to give advice (unless asked), and we will not attempt to set each other straight. We want to create a safe space to welcome our souls.

- We will not toot our own horn. Is what I want to share for the benefit of the group or self-serving?

- We will observe deep confidentiality. What is shared in this space and time is confidential.

- We will be present as fully as possible. This means really listening to what others have to share and not planning what I want to say while someone else is speaking. We will refrain from side conversations.

- We will invite others to share, not demand it. Be free to speak or not speak and know that you do it with our support.

- We will attempt to respond to each other with honest, open questions. (Some examples are: "What did you learn from that experience?" and "What did you mean when you said...?")

- We will not judge each other.

- We will honor silence. We will take time to reflect on what has been shared without immediately filling the space with words.[1]

Finally, a word about the format for your group. You might choose the chapters of this book as an outline covering a different topic each week. Feel free to use what works for you. If you want to change the order of the chapters, delete one or more–do what works best for your group. Be spontaneous. Remember, the goal of the group study is to live a more engaged life. Follow the promptings of your own heart and God's Spirit. Who knows where they will lead?

---

1   A number of these suggestions are based upon ideas found in *The Touchstones* formulated by the Center for Courage and Renewal (www.couragerenewal.org/touchstones).

Appendix B

Soul Print Exercise

Of all the soul descriptions I have encountered, none is as captivating as that put forward by Thomas Merton (1983), who compares the soul to a wild animal. Soul searching is like tracking a wild animal, you need to be still, silent, and not in a rush.

For this exercise, we will search for our "wild animal" by making a Soul Print Box. Put in five things that matter most to you. Possibly the greatest value of the Soul Print Box comes from the process of making it. In spiritual searches, process is often the most important thing. Let's view your Soul Print Box as a treasure chest of sorts, which makes filling the box a treasure hunt. In a treasure hunt, the two words are inseparable–to find a treasure you must hunt for it, and if you hunt, you will surely find a treasure. The very process of "boxing" your soul print–pulling together the significant signs of your soul–will help reveal your soul print. If you take the time to search for your home for soul print articles, you will be making the time to search for your soul. And if you hunt, you will surely find.

What do you put in your Soul Print Box? Love letters, family heirlooms, photographs, favorite quotes, and your own soul print reflections on life. If any items are too big, represent them with an object or write them on a slip of paper (Gafni 2001, p.24).

Another way to think of it is to imagine that a hurricane is about to hit your home and you have just 15 minutes to grab what is most important to you before you evacuate. What do you grab?

Bring your box to our first session and plan to share for about five minutes with the rest of the class on why these things are so important to you.

Appendix C

Story Telling Exercise

For next week's session, plan to share part of your life story. You'll have about five minutes. You can use the following questions inspired by the work of Frederic Hudson (1999) and Harvey Max Chochinov (2012) as a springboard for your sharing.

- If your life were a drama, what is the current *plot*? How did you get to be the way you are now?
- What are the significant *themes* of your story?
- What are the most important roles you have performed over the years? Why so?
- What have you done that gives you great satisfaction?
- Who are some of the important characters in your story? Why so?
- What are the major turning points of your story and how did you change?
- When have you felt most alive?
- What hopes do you have for your loved ones?
- What have you learned about living that you want to pass along to those you love?
- What would be the title of your life story?

Fairy Tale Exercise

Or if you prefer, write a fairy tale that describes your life. (This one is especially good if you have a particularly pressing problem right now.)

There will be three parts to your fairy tale:

1. *The description of the problem.* Do this using symbolic language, using animal (wolves, bears, etc.) or other fairy tale characters (princesses, shoe cobblers, knights, or kings). Let your current situation provide the inspiration, but as soon as you can, move away from your conscious awareness of the problem and let the story take over.

2. *The magical intervention.* Let your imagination come up with a magical solution–whether that's a potion, the arrival of a new character with special powers, a change in the weather, whatever comes to mind.

3. *The happy ever after.* Describe what it looks like when the problem is resolved.[1]

---

1   This idea was inspired by the work of Dana Gerhardt at http://mooncircles.com

Appendix D

Meditation on the Divine Connection

For next week's session, plan to share some photographs, art, or images of whatever connects you with the Divine–images that remind you of the immanence of the Divine.

You'll have about three minutes to share your images with the rest of the group and explain why they help you connect with God.

Appendix E

Blessing Exercise

As part of our effort to discover our life's meaning, we want to affirm each other's gifts. To this end you will draw the name of a class member and then reflect on *one* characteristic or attribute that person possesses that enriches our whole community. For example, maybe the name you draw is a person who is "dependable," always following through on their promises, or possibly they are "justice oriented," always looking out for the under-privileged. The idea is to notice this beautiful trait in one of our colleagues, and then you will have an opportunity to bring it forward to the group in a time of sharing. Plan to share for two or three minutes about what it is you see in this person that you admire, and why. You can write something out or speak from your heart. What matters is that your sharing about the honoree is authentic and honoring. Also, try to find a small token (something from around your home, or a small craft you make, or an inexpensive, under-$5 gift) to represent this attribute you see in your colleague and give it to them to remember this moment of acknowledgment. No one is to be left out.

To recap, you will draw the name of one of your classmates and then prepare prior to our next session:

- spoken words

- expressing an important gift the recipient brings to our community

- offering an active commitment to see that gift accepted and nurtured

- a small token to remember.

Appendix F

The Nine Contemplations of Atisha, Plus One

I would now like to share with you a famous Buddhist reflection on death, the Nine Contemplations of Atisha. The contemplations that follow offer a way for us, and those we serve, to explore the inevitability of death and what is important to us in the light of our mortality. The practice asks us to question what we are doing in our life at this very moment and to see what is important for us to do in order to prepare for death. The contemplations come from Atisha, an 11th-century Tibetan Buddhist scholar, who systematized the method for generating an enlightened mind. This exercise is based on the work of Roshi Joan Halifax and Larry Rosenberg (Halifax 1997).

As you prepare to go through these nine contemplations (plus one), it would be helpful to get comfortable, relax, secure a quiet environment, and have time to put the book down and reflect on what you read. Read in a *lectio divina* style. Don't hurry or rush through. Take your time and savor the experience. Pay attention to how your soul responds.

1. Death Is Inevitable

One day you are going to die. You cannot escape it. The time will come when you will no longer see the blueness of the sky, smell the freshness of the rain, or feel the warmth of breath deep in your belly.

Stop reading for a moment and let that thought really sink in. You are going to die.

Pain may or may not come as the different organs of your body begin to shut down and you can no longer enjoy the taste of food or even have the capacity to relieve yourself. This will happen. How does this make you feel? Afraid? "Fear is a natural reaction of moving closer to the truth", (Chödrön and Sell 2002, p.92). Where do you feel this sensation in your body right now?

All living things die. You will too. One translation from the Book of Ecclesiastes says, "Your days are few and you cannot know which will be your last. Appreciate the moment. Sharpen your mind. Live with attention. Live without expectation" (Shapiro 2000, p.51). You do not know which moment will be your last. How will you live now to minimize regrets for when that moment comes? How will you spend what moments you have remaining? How are you preparing for the death you will not escape?

It has been said that all life feeds on death. The food you ate earlier today–the vegetables, fruit, and meat absorbed by your body and providing nutrition for your continued existence–was recently alive. Death is required for life to continue. What life will your death nourish? (See Jenkinson 2015.)

This is the first contemplation–death is inevitable.

2. Life Span Is Decreasing Continuously

With each passing moment, the moment of your death draws nearer. Every breath you breathe brings you closer to your last. Every tick of the clock brings you closer to your final stroke.

Does this truth cause you to shut down in despair or motivate you to fully live now? What does living fully now mean to you? Experiencing as much pleasure as you can? Amassing possessions? Growing more powerful or famous? Will these help prepare you for your last moment? The profound question is: What makes your living meaningful? In light of your decreasing life span, how can you live meaningfully now to avoid regrets later?

Martin Luther King offers, "Life's most persistent and urgent question is, 'What are you doing for others?'" (1963, p.72). Cornell West adds, "What kind of human being do you want to be? What kind of legacy do you want to leave behind? What kind of witness do you want to bear?" (2008, p.28). What does living fully now mean to you?

How can you make the most of what moments you have left as you contemplate the reality that your life span is decreasing continuously?

3. Death Will Come, Whether or Not We Are Prepared for It

How can you prepare now for dying a good death? You wouldn't travel to another country without making some basic preparations. You would at least make sure you have a passport, appropriate clothes for the climate, and enough money for the trip.

Jesus admonishes us to not store up treasures on earth that moths will eat, rust will erode, or others will steal–but he says to store up treasures in heaven that can't be lost (Matthew 6.19-20, NIV). What does he mean?

In a world of impermanence, what truly lasts?

How are you spending the time you have now? What do you give your heart to? I have never met a dying person who has told me they wished they had gone to more football games, or spent more time shopping, or spent more time on the internet. Consider your personal calendar. How you spend your time reveals what you truly treasure.

Are there things you need to set right? Relational wounds you have put off attending to that continue to fester? Secrets that when found out will cause you or your loved ones shame? Financial dealings that will burden your family?

In companioning with nearly 2000 people who have died, here is what I've seen: those who cannot forgive themselves die hard; those who have, die easy. Which are you?

Remember, your death is coming whether you are prepared for it or not.

4. Human Life Expectancy Is Uncertain

"Is it realistic to wake up each day expecting to live?" (Jenkinson 2015, p.55). Most of the human beings alive right now have little hope that either they or their loved ones will live safely through the day. Famine, war, and disease are more real to them than to those of us in the insulated and privileged First World of the West. Is your living through this day certain?

There are more than seven billion human beings alive right at this moment. How many will die today? Will your name be on that list?

The second that muscle in the middle of your chest stops beating–it's all over. Stop for a second. Can you hear your heart? Can you sense its beat?

If you knew today would be your last day alive, how would you spend it? Who would you want to be with? What would you say to them? How do you feel? Sad or satisfied? Imagine that now in your mind's eye.

153

There's a verse in the New Testament which offers this observation: "Why, you do not even know what will happen tomorrow. What is your life? You are a mist that appears for a little while and then vanishes" (James 4.14, NIV).

There is no certainty that you will live to see the morrow. This is the fourth contemplation.

5. There Are Many Causes of Death

Cancer, Alzheimer's, being hit by a car, a hurricane, or a bullet–the possible causes of death are innumerable. Disease, accidents, violence, old age. One of them will get you. You can't dodge them all. The reality is there is simply no easy way to leave this planet.

One famous philosopher wrote, "We do not know where death awaits us: so let us wait for it everywhere. To practice death is to practice freedom. A man who has learned to die has unlearned how to be a slave" (Sogyal, Gaffney and Harvey 2002, p.15).

Most of the people I meet want to die quickly and peacefully in their sleep. While this may sound attractive, what about those who love you? How will they feel if they never get an opportunity to say goodbye? What if your last words were harsh? What if you die and they don't really know how much you care for them? Is that the way you want to leave?

Does knowing death may arrive in so many different ways close you down in fear? Does it fill you with anxiety? Or does it liberate you to live fully now, savoring every moment, every experience, every encounter with those you enjoy?

6. The Human Body Is Fragile and Vulnerable

If we are fortunate to grow old we learn just how fragile the human body is. Legs that carried us so well in our 20s and 30s can no longer be trusted. Simply having a bowel movement can become a cause for quiet celebration.

Our living is dependent on so many intricate and simple things. The beat of a heart. The ability to breathe. Digesting food. The loss of any one of these and you will soon be dead. Pause for a moment and focus your attention on your next breath. Feel the warmth enter deep into your lungs. Hold it for a few seconds and feel the sensation as you release. How many times a day do you do that without thought? Yet each is vital for your continued living.

From the moment of your first inhalation as a newborn to your last exhalation–all of life is a gift, a wonder. The vast number of sequential biological factors that have aligned for you to be alive, to be able to read these words, to know you are alive, is incalculable. Life is a miracle. You are a miracle.

What does such knowledge cause to arise in you?

Feel your next heartbeat. Savor your next breath. You are very fragile. And you are alive. How will you use this gift?

7. At the Time of Death, Our Material Resources Are Not of Use to Us

Close your eyes and imagine you are lying on your death bed. All of your energy has left. You can no longer move your legs or your arms. Trying to say a word or two takes a long time. The words are clear in your thoughts...you just can't seem to get them to cross your lips. Stay with that image for a few moments. How does it feel?

Turn your attention to all the life energy you have spent in amassing your most treasured possessions. Houses, cars, books, awards, gardens, artwork, collections, money–what good are they to you now? Can they help you in this moment of your dying?

Actually, they can get in the way. Attachments to things actually increase our suffering when we lose them. The summarizing wisdom to the Book of Ecclesiastes is: "The key to living well is remembering that nothing lasts" (Shapiro 2000, p.118).

The question is, how can you invest your time, your resources, and your energy now to prepare for the moment of your dying? What can you do now to prepare for a peaceful departure? Think on this. "Dying well is a bequest that you leave to those you love, probably the only thing that in the end will not be eaten by moths, apportioned by lawyers, or bought for quarters in a yard sale" (Jenkinson 2015, p.14).

What use are your most valued possessions as you lie dying?

8. Our Loved Ones Cannot Keep Us from Death

When the time comes, and it will, when you are dying–will there be loved ones there to care for you? The great likelihood is that you will need folks to help you as you come to the end. Will there be people who want to be there?

And if there are, how will you cope with the feeling of being a burden? That you are needy? That others you love will have to interrupt their lives to care for you? They may have to miss work. Leave their families or homes to care for you, to help you bathe, to toilet. You will be completely vulnerable and in need of care. Imagine this. And while their help will be needed, they cannot keep you from death, they can only ease its coming.

Letting go of your possessions may be difficult. Releasing those you love may be even more so. "As people come closer to death, I have found that only two questions really matter to them: 'Am I loved?' and 'Did I love well?'" (Ostaseski 2017, p.113). Close your eyes and picture the faces of those you hold most dear, one at a time. Will you be able to leave them? Will you be able to let go of those you love well?

The time will come when you need help, but even the aid of those who love you will not be able to keep you from death. This is the eighth contemplation.

9. Our Own Body Cannot Help Us at the Time of Our Death

Roshi Joan Halifax (1997) reminds us that since birth your body has been your most intimate friend. It has been the source of so much pleasure and pain. You have loved it, hated it, and at death you lose it. This body has been your true home for the entirety of your conscious existence. And now it is disintegrating. You are being dislocated from the protective shell that is deeply intertwined with who you are. You cannot stop it from happening. How does it feel?

Joseph Campbell tells us, "You don't understand death, you learn to acquiesce in death" (Campbell and Moyers 1988, p.151). With the loss of our body, maybe the last great lesson Death has to teach us is, how to surrender? Here we come face to face with the illusion what we are in control. We are not. We really never have been. Life is a gift. It comes and it goes. We cannot control it, we can only savor it.

All you have spent your lifetime in acquiring–your money, your treasures, your knowledge, your reputation, your relationships, and your health–all will vanish. In light of this fact, how will you live now to prepare for this moment?

These are the Nine Contemplations of Atisha:

1. Death is inevitable
2. Our life span is decreasing continuously
3. Death will come, whether or not we are prepared for it
4. Human life expectancy is uncertain
5. There are many causes of death
6. The human body is fragile and vulnerable
7. At the time of death, our material resources are not of use to us
8. Our loved ones cannot keep us from death
9. Our own body cannot help us at the time of our death.

(Gontag 2007)

Is that it? Is that all there is? Or is there more...?

Plus one: At the moment of your death, will you really be alone?

Think back over the most difficult moments of your life. The scariest events. Were you alone then? Or was there something deep inside you that helped you endure? Times when you believed all was lost, and yet you made it through? Was that unseen source of strength, that presence, was that your soul? Was it God? Is it with you now as you lie dying?

One of my favorite biblical passages is from the Letter to the Hebrews. It tells us:

> For God has said, I will not in any way fail you nor give you up nor leave you without support. I will not, I will not, I will not in any degree leave you helpless nor forsake nor let you down (relax my hold on you)! Assuredly not! (Hebrews 13.5, Amplified Bible)

At the moment of your death, will you really be alone?

References

Achterberg, J., B.M. Dossey and L. Kolkmeier (1994) *Rituals of Healing: Using Imagery for Health and Wellness*. New York: Bantam Books.

Barrett, D.B., G.T. Kurian and T.M. Johnson (2001) *World Christian Encyclopedia: A Comparative Survey of Churches and Religions in the Modern World*. Oxford and New York: Oxford University Press.

Baumeister, R.F., K.D. Vohs, J. Aaker and E.N. Garbinsky (2013) "Some key differences between a happy life and a meaningful life." *Journal of Positive Psychology* 8(6): 505-516.

Benson, P. and B. Spilka (1973) "God image as a function of self-esteem and locus of control." *Journal for the Scientific Study of Religion* 12(3): 297-310.

Berkson, M. (2016) *Death, Dying, and the Afterlife: Lessons from World Cultures, Course Guidebook*. Chantilly, VA: The Great Courses.

Bianchi, E.C. (1992) *Aging as a Spiritual Journey*. New York: Crossroad.

Biro, D. (2010) *The Language of Pain: Finding Words, Compassion, and Relief*. New York: W.W. Norton.

Blackler, L. (2017) "Hope for a miracle: treatment requests at the end of life." *Journal of Hospice and Palliative Nursing* 19(2): 120-121.

Borkowski, M. (2018) "The Question of Pain." *The New Inquiry*, July 5, 2012. Available at https://thenewinquiry.com/the-question-of-pain, accessed on March 31, 2018.

Boss, P. (1999) *Ambiguous Loss: Learning to Live with Unresolved Grief*. Cambridge, MA: Harvard University Press.

Bourdieu, P. (1989) "Social space and symbolic power." *Sociological Theory* 7(1): 14-25.

Bourdieu, P. (1996) "Physical space, social space and habitus." Vilhelm Aubert Memorial Lecture, Report 10, University of Oslo.

Breitbart, W. (2003) "Reframing hope: meaning-centered care for patients near the end of life. Interview by Karen S. Heller." *Journal of Palliative Medicine* 6(6): 979-988.

Breitbart, W., C. Gibson, S. Poppito and A. Berg (2004) "Psychotherapeutic interventions at the end of life: a focus on meaning and spirituality." *Canadian Journal of Psychiatry* 49(6): 366-372.

Buber, M. and W.A. Kaufmann (1970) *I and Thou*. New York: Scribner.

Buechner, F. (2016) *Buechner 101: Essays and Sermons by Frederick Buechner*. Cambridge, MA: Frederick Buechner Center.

Campbell, J. (2008) *The Hero with a Thousand Faces*. Novato, CA: New World Library.

Campbell, J. and B.D. Moyers (1988) *The Power of Myth*. New York: Doubleday.

Chittister, J. (2003) *Scarred by Struggle, Transformed by Hope*. Grand Rapids, ML: William B. Eerdmans and Ottawa Novalis, Saint Paul University.

Chochinov, H.M. (2012) *Dignity Therapy: Final Words for Final Days*. Oxford and New York: Oxford University Press.

Chödrön, P. and E.H. Sell (2002) *Comfortable with Uncertainty: 108 Teachings*. Boston, MA: Shambhala.

Connor, S.R., B. Pyenson, K. Fitch, C. Spence and K. Iwasaki (2007) "Comparing hospice and nonhospice patient survival among patients who die within a three-year window." *Journal of Pain and Symptom Management* 33(3): 238–246.

Cousineau, P. (1998) *The Art of Pilgrimage: The Seeker's Guide to Making Travel Sacred*. Berkeley, CA: Conari Press.

Cubanski, J., T. Neuman, S. Griffin and A. Damico (2016) "Medicare Spending at the End of Life: A Snapshot of Beneficiaries Who Died in 2014 and the Cost of Their Care." Retrieved January 9, 2018 from www.kff.org/report-section/medicare-spending-at-the-end-of-life-introduction/#endnote_link_192976-5

Douglas-Klotz, N. (1990) *Prayers of the Cosmos: Meditations on the Aramaic Words of Jesus*. San Francisco: Harper & Row.

Evans, A.R. (2011) *Is God Still at the Bedside? The Medical, Ethical, and Pastoral Issues of Death and Dying*. Grand Rapids, MI: William B. Eerdmans Pub. Co.

Frankl, V.E. (1984) *Man's Search for Meaning*. New York: Pocket Books.

Friedman, E.H. (2011) *Generation to Generation: Family Process in Church and Synagogue*. New York: Guilford Press.

Gafni, M. (2001) *Soul Prints: Your Path to Fulfillment*. New York: Pocket Books.

Gontag, O. (2007) "The Nine Contemplations of Atisha." Retrieved October 27, 2017 from www.mindfulness.com/2007/10/30/the-nine-contemplations-of-atisha

Gorsuch, R.L. and A. Wong-McDonald (2004) "A multivariate theory of God concept, religious motivation, locus of control, coping, and spiritual well-being." *Journal of Psychology and Theology* 32(4): 318–334.

Grewe, F. (2013) "Healing in hospice." *PlainViews* 10: 5.

Grewe, F. (2014) *What the Dying Have Taught Me about Living: The Awful Amazing Grace of God*. Cleveland, OH: Pilgrim Press.

Grewe, F. (2016) "The soul's legacy: a program designed to help prepare senior adults cope with end-of-life existential distress." *Journal of Health Care Chaplaincy* 23(1): 1–14.

Halifax, J. (1997) "The Nine Contemplations of Atisha." *Being with Dying*. Louisville, CO: Sounds True.

Hall, J.A. (1983) *Jungian Dream Interpretation: A Handbook of Theory and Practice*. Toronto, Canada: Inner City Books.

Hanh, Thich Nhat (1999) *The Heart of the Buddha's Teaching. Transforming Suffering into Peace, Joy and Liberation: The Four Noble Truths, the Noble Eightfold Path, and Other Basic Buddhist Teachings*. New York: Broadway Books.

Heschel, A.J. (1965) *Who is Man?* Stanford, CA: Stanford University Press.

Hester, D.M. (2010) *End-of-Life Care and Pragmatic Decision Making: A Bioethical Perspective.* Cambridge and New York: Cambridge University Press.

Hudson, F.M. (1999) *The Adult Years: Mastering the Art of Self-Renewal.* San Francisco: Jossey-Bass.

Jenkinson, S. (2015) *Die Wise: A Manifesto for Sanity and Soul.* Berkley, CA: North Atlantic Books.

Kerr, H. (1988) "Preacher, professor, editor." *Theology Today* 45(1): 1-4.

King Jr., M.L. (1963) *Strength to Love.* New York: Harper & Row.

King, M.L., C. Carson and P. Holloran (1998) *A Knock at Midnight: Inspiration from the Great Sermons of Reverend Martin Luther King, Jr.* New York: Intellectual Properties Management in association with Warner Books.

Kleinman, A. (1980) *Patients and Healers in the Context of Culture: An Exploration of the Borderland between Anthropology, Medicine, and Psychiatry.* Berkeley: University of California Press.

Kunkel, M.A., S. Cook, D.S. Meshel, D. Daughtry and A. Hauenstein (1999) "God images: a concept map." *Journal for the Scientific Study of Religion* 38(2): 193-202.

Kurtz, E. and K. Ketcham (1992) *The Spirituality of Imperfection: Modern Wisdom from Classic Stories.* New York: Bantam Books.

Lane, B.C. (2002) *Landscapes of the Sacred: Geography and Narrative in American Spirituality.* Baltimore, MD: Johns Hopkins University Press.

Lane, B.C. (2007) *The Solace of Fierce Landscapes: Exploring Desert and Mountain Spirituality.* Oxford and New York: Oxford University Press.

Lizza, J.P. (2006) *Persons, Humanity, and the Definition of Death.* Baltimore, MD: Johns Hopkins University Press.

Lynn, J., J.K. Harrold and J.L. Schuster (2011) *Handbook for Mortals: Guidance for People Facing Serious Illness.* New York: Oxford University Press.

Manning, B. (1990) *The Ragamuffin Gospel: Good News for the Bedraggled, Beat-up, and Burnt Out.* Portland, OR: Multnomah.

Manning, B. (2000) *Ruthless Trust: The Ragamuffin's Path to God.* San Francisco: HarperSanFrancisco.

Marty, M. (1988) "Religion and healing: the four expectations." *Second Opinion* March(7): 60-80.

Merton, M. (1968) *Conjectures of a Guilty Bystander.* Garden City, NY: Image.

Merton, T. (1973) *The Asian Journal of Thomas Merton.* New York: New Directions Pub. Corp.

Merton, T. (1976) *Disputed Questions.* New York: Noonday.

Merton, T. (1983) "The inner experience: notes on contemplation (I)." *Cistercian Studies Quarterly* 18(1): 3-15.

Merton, T. (2003) *New Seeds of Contemplation.* Boston: Shambhala.

Mohrmann, M.E. (1995) *Medicine as Ministry: Reflections on Suffering, Ethics, and Hope.* Cleveland, OH: Pilgrim Press.

Moore, T. (1992) *Care of the Soul: A Guide for Cultivating Depth and Sacredness in Everyday Life.* New York: HarperCollins.

Moyers, B. (2000) "Part 2: A Different Kind of Care." *On Our Own Terms: Moyers on Dying*. New York: Public Affairs Television and PBS Thirteen, WNET, DVD.

Muramoto, O. (2017) "Re-emerging Ethical Challenges over the Determination of Death: Legal Mandate, Medical Science, Social Unity, or Personal Choice." (Presentation at conference, Emerging Issues in Bioethics and Government: Facing Ethical Challenges and Finding Solutions, Salem, OR, May 19.)

Murphy, N.C. (2006) *Bodies and Souls, or Spirited Bodies?* Cambridge, UK and New York: Cambridge University Press.

Murphy, P. (2013) "Healing Suffering: Identifying and Treating Spiritual Distress." (Lecture, Providence Hospital, Medford, OR, January 25.)

Murray, K. (2012) "Why doctors die differently." *The Wall Street Journal*, February 25.

Nagy, E. (2008) "Innate intersubjectivity: newborn's sensitivity to communication disturbance." *Developmental Psychology* 44(6): 1779-1784.

Nouwen, H.J.M. (1986) *Reaching Out: The Three Movements of the Spiritual Life*. Garden City, NY: Image Books.

Nouwen, H.J.M. (1997) *Mornings with Henri J.M. Nouwen: Readings and Reflections*. Ann Arbor, MI: Charis Books.

Nouwen, H.J.M. (2010) *The Wounded Healer: Ministry in Contemporary Society*. Garden City, NY: Image Doubleday.

Nouwen, H.J.M. and R. Durback (1989) *Seeds of Hope: A Henri Nouwen Reader*. Toronto and New York: Bantam Books.

O'Donohue, J. (2008) *To Bless the Space between Us: A Book of Blessings*. New York: Doubleday.

O'Donohue, J. (2012) *Imagination as the Path of the Spirit*. Oxford: Greenbelt (audio recording).

Oregon Health Authority (2017) *Oregon Death with Dignity Act: Data Summary 2016*. Retrieved July 29, 2017 from www.oregon.gov/oha/PH/PROVIDERPARTNER RESOURCES/EVALUATIONRESEARCH/DEATHWITHDIGNITYACT/Documents/ year19.pdf

Ornstein, K.A., M.D. Aldridge, M.M. Garrido, R. Gorges, D.E. Meier and A.S. Kelley (2015) "Association between hospice use and depressive symptoms in surviving spouses." *JAMA Internal Medicine* 175(7): 1138-1146.

Ostaseski, F. (2017) *The Five Invitations: Discovering What Death Can Teach Us about Living Fully*. New York: Flatiron Books.

Palmer, P.J. (2008) *A Hidden Wholeness: The Journey toward an Undivided Life*. San Francisco: Jossey-Bass.

Pearson, L. (1969) *Death and Dying: Current Issues in the Treatment of the Dying Person*. Cleveland, OH: Case Western Reserve University.

Phelps, A.C., P.K. Maciejewski, M. Nilsson, T.A. Balboni *et al.* (2009) "Association between religious coping and use of intensive life-prolonging care near death among patients with advanced cancer." *JAMA* 301(11): 1140-1147.

Pilch, J.J. (2000) *Healing in the New Testament: Insights from Medical and Mediterranean Anthropology*. Augsburg Fortress, MN: Fortress Press.

Plato and B. Jowett (1930) *The Phaedo of Plato*. Waltham Saint Lawrence, Berkshire: Golden Cockerel Press.

Puchalski, C. and B. Ferrell (2010) *Making Health Care Whole: Integrating Spirituality into Patient Care*. West Conshohocken, PA: Templeton Press.

Puchalski, C., B. Ferrell, R. Virani, S. Otis-Green *et al.* (2009) "Improving the quality of spiritual care as a dimension of palliative care: the report of the Consensus Conference." *Journal of Palliative Medicine* 12(10): 885-904.

Pyenson, B., S. Connor, K. Fitch and B. Kinzbrunner (2004) "Medicare cost in matched hospice and non-hospice cohorts." *Journal of Pain and Symptom Management* 28(3): 200-210.

Rahner, K. and J. Griffiths (1980) *Prayers and Meditations: An Anthology of the Spiritual Writings by Karl Rahner.* New York: Seabury Press.

Rogers, C.R. (1995) *A Way of Being.* Boston: Houghton Mifflin.

Sanders, J.J., V. Chow, A.C. Enzinger, T.C. Lam *et al.* (2017) "Seeking and accepting: U.S. clergy theological and moral perspectives informing decision making at the end of life." *Journal of Palliative Medicine* 20(10): 1059-1067.

Sani, F. (ed.) (2008) *Self Continuity: Individual and Collective Perspectives.* New York: Psychology Press.

Shapiro, R.M. (2000) *The Way of Solomon: Finding Joy and Contentment in the Wisdom of Ecclesiastes.* San Francisco: HarperSanFrancisco.

Siegel, R.D. (2014) *The Science of Mindfulness: A Research-Based Path to Well-Being.* Course Guidebook. Chantilly, VA: The Great Courses.

Smalley, G. and J. Trent (1998) *The Gift of the Blessing/The Gift of Honor.* New York: Inspirational Press.

Sogyal, R., P. Gaffney and A. Harvey (2002) *The Tibetan Book of Living and Dying* (rev. and updated ed.). San Francisco, CA: HarperSanFrancisco.

Solomon, R. (2000) "Lecture 16: Heidegger on the World and the Self." *No Excuses: Existentialism and the Meaning of Life* (CD). Chantilly, VA: The Teaching Company.

Span, P. (2014) "When advance directives are ignored." *The New York Times,* June 24. Retrieved January 23, 2018 from https://newoldage.blogs.nytimes.com/2014/06/24/when-advance-directives-are-ignored/?mcubz=2

Steinhauser, K.E., H.B. Bosworth, E.C. Clipp, M. McNeilly *et al.* (2002) "Initial assessment of a new instrument to measure quality of life at the end of life." *Journal of Palliative Medicine* 5(6): 829-841.

Steinhauser, K.E., N.A. Christakis, E.C. Clipp, M. McNeilly *et al.* (2001) "Preparing for the end of life: preferences of patients, families, physicians, and other care providers." *Journal of Pain and Symptom Management* 22(3): 727-737.

Tippett, K. (2007) *On Being: The Miracle of Reconciliation.* National Public Radio. First broadcast March 22, 2007. Retrieved January 23, 2018 from https://onbeing.org/blog/krista-tippett-the-miracle-of-reconciliation

West, C. (2008) *Hope on a Tightrope: Words & Wisdom.* Carlsbad, CA: Smiley Books.

WHO (World Health Organization) (1946) *Preamble to the Constitution of the World Health Organization.* (International Health Conference, New York.)

Willard, D. (1998) *The Divine Conspiracy: Rediscovering Our Hidden Life in God.* San Francisco: HarperSanFrancisco.

Wiman, C. (2013) *My Bright Abyss: Meditation of a Modern Believer.* New York: Farrar, Straus and Giroux.

Wong, P.T.P. (ed.) (2012) *The Human Quest for Meaning: Theories, Research, and Applications.* Personality and Clinical Psychology Series. New York: Routledge.

Yalom, I.D. (1980) *Existential Psychotherapy.* New York: Basic Books.

Zitter, J.N. (2014) "Food and the dying patient." *The New York Times,* August 21.

Subject Index

life expectancy, uncertainty of 153-4
life review 51, 55
logotherapy 40, 45
losses 57

material possessions 155
meaning
  feeling useful 46
  fluidity of 45
  global 45
  loss of 30-3
  making 45-6
  "more time for what?" question
    32-3, 153-4
  requires relationship with others
    42-4, 53
  in serving others 30-1
  situational 45
  takes on importance/urgency 40
meditation
  on the divine connection 131, 149
  nine contemplations of Atisha 133,
    151-7
  soul 67
meta-narrative 69-70, 76-7
midwife metaphor 57
mirror reflection 43
monergistic belief system 82
"more time for what?" question 32-3,
  153-4
mythology, cultural 74-5

narrative, meta- 69-70, 76-7
needy, fear of being 31, 35-6, 76
neighborhood, vs. brotherhood 90-1
nine contemplations of Atisha 133,
  151-7
non-reductionalist physicalism 61-2
non-verbal communication 37-8

orientation-disorientation-
  reorientation process 77

pain
  analgesics for 41
  definition of 41
  effective change agent 24-5
  quintessential private experience
    27
paradox of dying well 115-6
pastoral care teams 120
POLST (Physician's Orders for Life-
  Sustaining Treatment) 123
positive God image 81
priorities, rearrangement of 33-4

readiness for hospice care 118-9
reality, surrendering to 46-7, 156-7
reflection 42-3
relationship
  meaning and 42-4, 53
  vulnerability and 36-7, 113

safe space, creating 57
Saunders, Dame Cicely 13
self-image, "god" selected in 81
seminar program 51
"should," avoid use of 59
silence 37-8
Sisyphus myth 29
situational meaning 45
social habitus 74
social media 104
soul
  defining the term 61-3
  leaving the body 60-1
  wild animal metaphor 63, 66
soul legacy
  definition of 55
  form of 55
  unique personal blessing in 55
Soul Legacy Seminar program 128-37
  see also group study
soul meditation 67
Soul Print Box 65-6, 129, 146
specialness (defense strategy) 34, 47
spiritual triangulation 116-7

Author Index